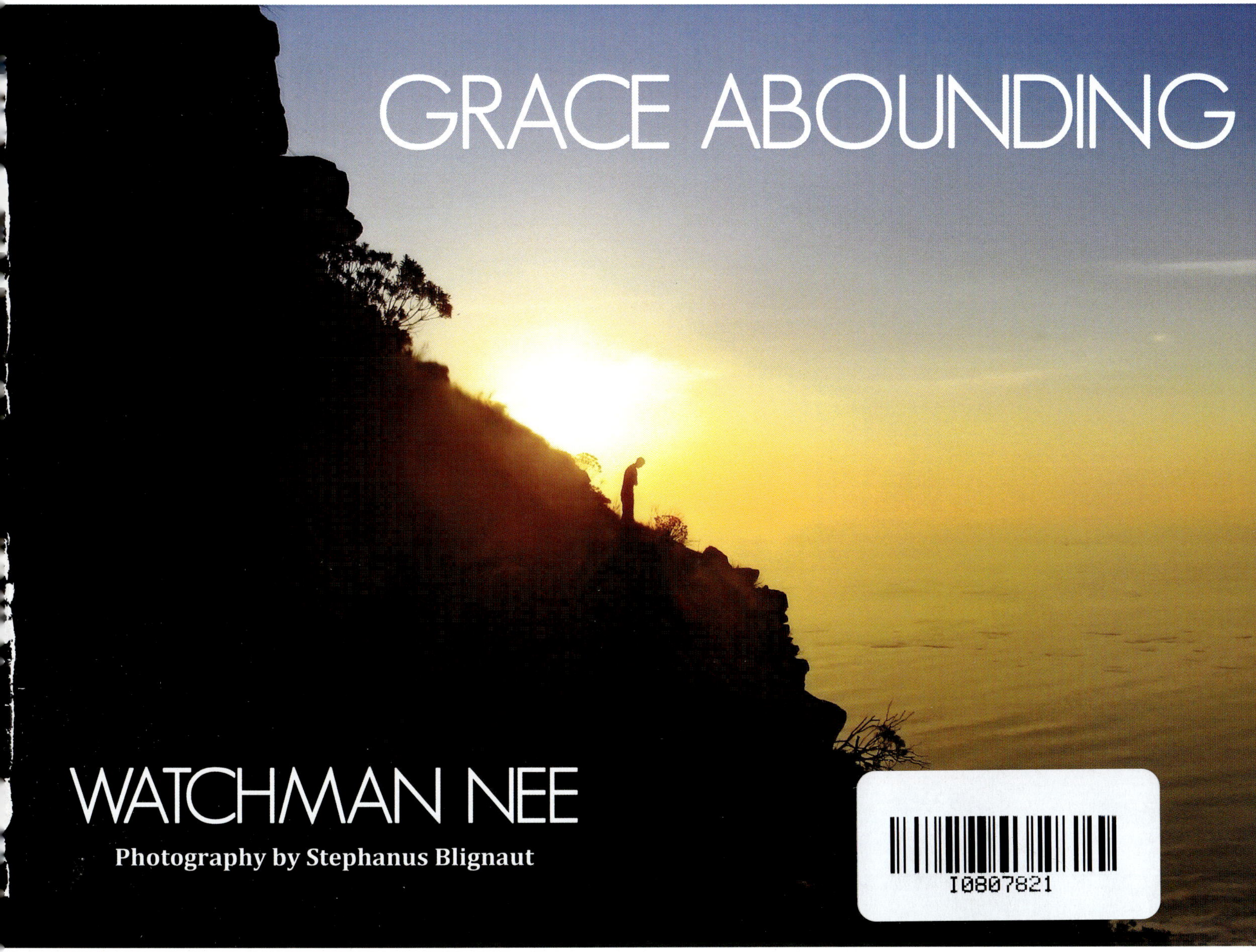

GRACE ABOUNDING

WATCHMAN NEE

Photography by Stephanus Blignaut

Namibian Desert

GRACE ABOUNDING

... where sin abounded grace has overabounded.
Romans 5:20

WATCHMAN NEE

Tradouss Mountain Pass, Western Cape

All pictures were taken in Southern Africa. The cover photo is from the upper slopes of Lion's Head in Capetown.

Grace Abounding

by Watchman Nee

ISBN: 978-1-68062-076-4

Available from the Publishers at:
11515 Allecingie Parkway
Richmond, Virginia 23235

Unless otherwise indicated,
All Scripture quotations are from the
American Standard Version 1901.

Printed in the United States of America

Sheep in the Great Black Mountains, Oudtshoorn

Fear not, little flock; for it is your Father's good pleasure to give you the kingdom.

Luke 12:32

Preface

After hearing the testimony of Stephanus Blignaut and his burden for this book we were greatly encouraged and wanted to help. He and his wife have used their own photographs alongside with some of the writings of Watchman Nee that have been the most helpful to them. Here is a portion of his testimony shared with us:

> "For twenty years I've been a missionary but sadly have worked unknowingly on an unhealthy legal side through the deception of the old man. But early in 2012 The Lord graciously brought me into a crisis where I became convinced that I was losing my life through sickness. And was confronted by The Lord in the reality of last moments on earth whether the Gospel I used to preach was truly good enough to die by. And as I slowly observed I was busy leaving my wife and children I realized I was in a spiritual desert and in this crisis was in need of help myself. This was a lonely and frightening time. Then I saw a little book on our bookshelf that I had purchased in a second hand bookshop but never read it, the book Sit Walk Stand. Seeing the title of the book I thought, "how much more basic can you get? And I feel the need of the basics again." So I started reading the book with my life in a crisis. And the book challenged my entire view of the Gospel which was rather legal at the point. But that precious book opened my eyes to the reality of our position in Christ. After so much blessing by Watchman Nee, I turned to another book on the shelf which I had obtained the same way but never read. We only had the one book of the six volume series, only the fourth one, Not I But Christ. But in this book The Lord greatly ministered to me through the chapters, If Any Man Sin, Deliverance, and Not I But Christ. Through all of these the Lord rectified some very wrong thinking I used to have and could not understand how I made the error. But I received light on how I made this error when I read the next book The Spiritual Man in seeing the deception and operation of the old man. I knew that I was born again, I am still convinced that I was born again but somehow sadly missed for twenty years the true and full Christian life. I further could not understand how since my rebirth in 1992 I have never heard this message preached by anyone. What a famine there is in our preaching!"

His desire to piece together 31 days of morning and evening ministries was that they could be used in a devotional way throughout a month. With others this may be something to occasionally pickup off of the coffee table and read at just the right time. There is a type of spiritual progress to be found through the book and yet any portion seems to stand by itself and a supply of life for all of us.

May the Lord himself encourage all of us through the pages of this book just as He did the one who compiled it.

Christian Fellowship Publishers

Aloe ferox in the Black Mountains in Southern Africa.

For of his fulness we all received, and grace for grace.

John 1:16

A Note from the Photographer & Compiler

We want to deeply thank Christian Fellowship Publishers for the opportunity they granted us to present the readers with this book to lift up Christ Jesus once more and to combine the writings of Watchman Nee with the beautiful nature of our Creator. We pray that it truly will be a blessing to everyone that reads through the pages of this devotional.

We also want to, in a very special way, thank CFP for their faithfulness in the service of the Lord over so many, many years. Through this faithful ministry of CFP the Lord has done a wonderful work for me and my family by opening our eyes and leading us to much greater depth through His grace. That is why we want to call this book *Grace Abounding*. And indeed how grateful I am for the utterly firm foundation that I can lay for my children and their children's children till the day of the Lord through the ministry of brother Watchman Nee whom the Lord has used so powerfully. Thank you CFP for faithfully making sure that these great teachings of brother Watchman Nee keep blessing men and women all over the world. Brothers, God bless you in your daily work.

I would also like to thank my wife, Rose, for all the many, many hours and days and weeks and months we sat together doing the reading, picture editing, layout and planning and doing all the technical work on the computer. Without you it would be totally impossible. And I am so thankful that the Lord has given me such a perfect helpmeet and a great encouragement. Thank you my dear wife.

Thank the Lord for leading the way in giving us the vision and opening the doors for being able to compile this book and minister to fellow brothers, sisters and friends all over the world. May the Lord continue to use this ministry in thousands upon thousands of lives through all the different books that have already been published.

We are furthermore so thankful to the Lord. I think everyone that is washed in the blood can shout Amen and praises to the Lord, because He, our God, is the one who backs His own word by His faithfulness. He is the power and strength of all that He speaks. He *is* life, our life-Giver and the One who will keep us to the last day. May He use the pages of this book to bring life in the hearts of all serious men and women of God. Glory be to the Lord for giving us His faithful servants like brother Watchman Nee. Thank you, Lord!

Stephanus Blignaut, South Africa

Day 1–Morning

Vanrynevelds Pass Dam, Graaff-Reinet

... know ye not that the friendship of the world is enmity with God? Whosoever therefore would be a friend of the world maketh himself an enemy of God.

James 4:4

Salvation–A Change of Position

Taken from the book: **A Living Sacrifice**

It is imperative for us to understand man's state before God. People of the world today need not do anything to cause them to perish. No one is required to kill in order to perish; nor by not killing will any be spared from perdition. The whole world is perishing, but God is pulling out some from among the perishing. So far as the whole world is concerned, it is already damned; but so far as individuals are concerned, this one and that one are being saved. It is not separating a flock of one hundred into fifty sheep and fifty goats; rather, it is netting some fish out of a sea of fish. All those that are caught in the net are saved while those that remain in the sea are yet lost.

Therefore, in answering the question of whether one is saved or lost, the issue does not rest on one's personal conduct; it is instead settled by the person's whereabouts. If he is in the boat, he is saved; if he is still in the sea, he is lost. It makes no difference if one is good or bad, a gentleman or a villain, with or without conscience. As long as he is in the world, he is lost. If he has not come out, has not left that place which is under judgment, he is a condemned sinner.

"For as through the one man's disobedience (Adam's) the many were made sinners" (Romans 5:19). It is not necessary for a person to sin in order to be qualified as a sinner. Because of one man's sin, all have been constituted sinners. As long as the person is in Adam, that is, in the world, he stands opposite to God, and is therefore an enemy of God. His position is wrong, for it is a lost position. This, then, is the story of the unsaved.

Day 1–Evening

Cloud blanket covering the tips of the Great Black Mountains

For the wages of sin is death; but the free gift of God is eternal life in Christ Jesus our Lord.

Romans 6:23

Spiritually Dead

Taken from the book: **The Spiritual Man, Vol. I**

Adam lived by the breath of life becoming spirit in him. By the spirit he sensed God, knew God's voice, and communed with God. He had a very keen awareness of God. But after his fall his spirit died.

When God spoke to Adam at the first He said, "in the day that you eat of it (the fruit of the tree of good and evil) you shall die" (Genesis 2:17). Adam and Eve nevertheless continued on for hundreds of years after eating the forbidden fruit. This obviously indicates that the death God foretold was not physical. Adam's death began in his spirit.

What really is death? According to its scientific definition, death is "the cessation of communication with environment." Death of the spirit is the cessation of its communication with God. Death of the body is the cutting off of communication between spirit and body. So when we say the spirit is dead it does not imply there is no more spirit; we simply mean the spirit has lost its sensitivity towards God and thus is dead to Him. The exact situation is that the spirit is incapacitated, unable to commune with God....

He still had his spirit, yet it was dead to God for it had lost its spiritual instinct. It is still so; sin has destroyed the spirit's keen intuitive knowledge of God and rendered man spiritually dead. He may be religious, moral, learned, capable, strong and wise, but he is dead to God. He may even talk about God, reason about God and preach God, but he is still dead to Him. Man is not able to hear or to sense the voice of God's Spirit. Consequently in the New Testament God often refers to those who are living in the flesh as dead.

Day 2–Morning

The wonder rock in the tips of the Great Black Mountains

Jesus answered and said unto him, Verily, verily, I say unto thee, Except a man be born again, he cannot see the kingdom of God.

John 3:3 KJV

Born Again

Taken from the book: **The Spiritual Man, Vol. I**

The concept of regeneration as found in the Bible speaks of the process of passing out of death into life. A man's spirit before regeneration is far away from God and is considered dead, for death is dissociation from life and from God Who is the fountain of life. Death is hence separation from God. Man's spirit is dead and therefore unable to commune with Him. Either his soul controls him and plunges him into a life of ideas and imaginations, or the lusts and habits of his body stimulate him and reduce his soul to servitude.

Man's spirit needs to be quickened because it is born dead. The new birth which the Lord Jesus spoke about to Nicodemus is the new birth of the spirit. It certainly is not a physical birth as Nicodemus suspected, nor is it a soulical one. We must note carefully that new birth imparts God's life to the spirit of man. Inasmuch as Christ has atoned for our soul and destroyed the principle of the flesh, so we who are joined to Him participate in His resurrection life. We have been united with Him in His death; consequently it is in our spirit that we first reap the realization of His resurrection life. New birth is something which happens entirely within the spirit; it has no relation to soul or body. ...

The writer of Proverbs tells us that "the spirit of man is the lamp of the Lord" (20:27). During the time of regeneration the Holy Spirit comes into man's spirit and quickens it as though kindling a lamp. This is the "new spirit" mentioned in Ezekiel 36:26; the dead old spirit is quickened into life when the Holy Spirit infuses it with God's uncreated life. Before regeneration the soul of man is in control of his spirit while his own "self' rules his soul and his passion governs his body. Soul has become the life of the body.

At regeneration man receives God's own life into his spirit and is born of God. As a consequence, the Holy Spirit now rules man's spirit which in turn is equipped to regain control over the soul and, through the soul, to govern his body. Because the Holy Spirit becomes the life of man's spirit, the latter becomes the life of man's whole being. The spirit, soul and body are restored to God's original intention in every born-again person.

Day 2–Evening

From the top of Table Mountain overviewing the western shore of the Cape Peninsula

My Spirit shall not always plead with Man; for he indeed is flesh.

Genesis 6:3 Darby

Vanity of Vanities

Taken from the book: **The Spiritual Man, Vol. I**

I Corinthians 2:14 speaks of such unregenerated persons in this fashion: "The natural (soulish) man does not receive the gifts of the spirit of God, for they are folly to him, and he is not able to understand them because they are spiritually discerned." Such men as are under the control of their souls with their spirits suppressed are in direct contrast to spiritual people. They may be exceedingly intelligent, able to present masterful ideas or theories, yet they do not consent to the things of the Spirit of God. They are unfit to receive revelation from the Holy Spirit. Such revelation is vastly different from human ideas. Man may think human intellect and reasoning are almighty, that the brain is able to comprehend all truths of the world; but the verdict of God's Word is, "vanity of vanities."

While man is in his soulish state he frequently senses the insecurity of this age and so he too seeks the eternal life of the coming age. But even if he does, he is still powerless to uncover the Word of life by his much thinking and theorizing. How untrustworthy are human reasonings! We often observe how very clever persons clash in their different opinions. Theories easily lead man into error. They are castles in the air, tumbling him into eternal darkness.

How true it is that without the guidance of the Holy Spirit intellect not only is undependable but also extremely dangerous, because it often confuses the issue of right and wrong. A slight carelessness may cause not merely temporary loss but even everlasting harm. The darkened mind of man frequently leads him to eternal death. If only unregenerated souls could see this, how good it would be!

In yielding to the demand of its passions and lusts the soul has become a slave to the body so that the Holy Spirit finds it useless to strive for God's place in such a one. Hence the Scripture declares, "My Spirit shall not always plead with Man; for he indeed is flesh" (Genesis 6:3 Darby)

Day 3—Morning

Sunset in the Overberg area in the most southern tip of Africa

Verily, verily, I say unto you, He that heareth my word, and believeth him that sent me, hath eternal life, and cometh not into judgment, but hath passed out of death into life. John 5:24

Christ Our Substitute

Taken from the book: **The Spiritual Man, Vol. I**

Death has permeated the spirit, soul and body of all men; there is no part of a human being into which it has not found its way. It is therefore imperative that man receive God's life. The way of salvation cannot be in human reform, for "death" is irreparable. Sin must be judged before there can be rescue out of death. Exactly this is what has been provided by the salvation of the Lord Jesus.

The man who sins must die. This is announced in the Bible. No animal nor angel can suffer the penalty of sin in man's stead. It is man's triune nature [spirit, soul, and body] which sins, therefore it is man who must die. Only humanity can atone for humanity. But because sin is in his humanity, man's own death cannot atone for his sin. The Lord Jesus came and took human nature upon himself in order that He might be judged instead of humanity. Untainted by sin, His holy human nature could therefore through death atone for sinful humanity. He died a substitute, suffered all penalty of sin, and offered his life a ransom for many. Consequently, whoever believes on Him shall be judged no more (John 5:24).

When the Word became flesh He included all flesh in himself. As the action of one man, Adam, represents the action of all mankind, so the work of one man, Christ, represents the work of all. We must see how inclusive Christ is before we can understand what redemption is. Why is it that the sin of one man, Adam, is judged to be the sin of all men both present and past? Because Adam is humanity's head from whom all other men have come into the world. Similarly the obedience of one man, Christ, becomes the righteousness of many, both of the present and the past, inasmuch as Christ constitutes the head of a new mankind entered into by a new birth.

Day 3–Evening

False Bay looking towards the Kogel Mountains at the Cape of Good Hope

But of him are ye in Christ Jesus, who was made unto us wisdom from God, and righteousness and sanctification, and redemption.

I Corinthians 1:30

Our Righteousness

Taken from the book: **The Glory of His Life**

Suppose we imagine ourselves asking a brother who knows the word of God: "Will your righteousness ever fail?" He will answer, "No, never." "But will your conduct ever fail?" we may ask. He will say, "Certainly." Do you see that his righteousness will never fail, though his conduct may? His righteousness is not his conduct. If this were true, then when his conduct failed, his righteousness would fail too. Yet his righteousness is not his conduct, it is not that which is subject to failure; his righteousness is the Christ who never fails. And so our righteousness too never fails; it is as unfailing as Christ is. Now this may sound too bold, but it is the word of God. Our righteousness is Christ. Because He never fails, our righteousness never fails either.

Some may perhaps inquire, Does it then mean that our bad conduct does not matter? It definitely does matter. For the Bible shows us that a Christian has two garments: one is the Lord Jesus, for He is our robe, He is our righteousness; the other is the bright and pure fine linen of Revelation 19:8: "For the fine linen is the righteous acts of the saints." ("Righteous acts" is "righteousnesses" in the original, meaning the many acts of righteousness.) All the good conduct of a Christian—all his outward righteousnesses—come from grace as a result of the working of the Holy Spirit in him; they are not something which he has naturally. As we approach God we are not naked, because we are clothed with Christ who is our righteousness. However, as we appear before the judgment seat of Christ we must bring our own righteousness, that which is called the righteousnesses of the saints (see II Corinthians 5:10, I Corinthians 4:5).

Day 4–Morning

The Pinnacles of Graaff-Reinet

Him who knew no sin he made to be sin on our behalf; that we might become the righteousness of God in him.

II Corinthians 5:21

The Righteousness of God

Taken from the book: **The Glory of His Life**

There is one name in the Old Testament which is very precious. It is "Jehovah our righteousness" (Jeremiah 23:6, 33:16). Jehovah is our righteousness, therefore our righteousness is not our conduct. May God open our eyes that we may see the gospel, even the foundation of the gospel. As we come to God, Christ—not our conduct—is our righteousness. The Lord is our righteousness. We come to Him through Christ. What else is as firm and immovable as this? ...

We will now consider the third matter, which is found in II Corinthians 5:21: "Him who knew no sin he made to be sin on our behalf; that we might become the righteousness of God." We who sinned are saved because Christ was made sin for us. We who are saved through the work of Christ have now become the righteousness of God in Him. This is a direct complement to I Corinthians 1:30. There we see that "Christ became our righteousness"; here in II Corinthians we find that "we become the righteousness of God." Whoever acknowledges the One that was without sin and yet was made sin for us becomes himself the righteousness of God.

We do not know how to say it, for it is truly most wonderful: we become the righteousness of God! The Bible tells us that our righteousness is Christ and God's righteousness is we ourselves. God has made Christ our righteousness, He has also made us His righteousness in Christ. What does it mean by our becoming the righteousness of God? It means that if anyone wants to learn and to see the righteousness of God, he need only find a Christian, for it is expressed in the life of a Christian. For this reason, a Christian is the righteousness of God.

Before we believe in the Lord we are blind to God's standards for righteousness and unrighteousness. But even after we become Christians, we may still be confused in identifying what is righteous and what is unrighteous. God will therefore not only save us but also teach us the lesson on righteousness. In His redemption He not only saves the unrighteous but He also instructs us as to what righteousness is.

Day 4–Evening

Cape L'Agullus, Struis Bay

For God so loved the world, that He gave His only begotten Son, that whosoever believeth in Him should not perish, but have everlasting life.

John 3:16 KJV

Born Anew

Taken from the book: **The Spiritual Man, Vol. I**

What then must one do to be born anew in one's spirit? We know that the Lord Jesus died in the sinner's place. He suffered in His body on the cross for all the sins of the world. God views the death of the Lord Jesus as the death of all the world's people. His holy humanity suffered death for all unholy humanity. But something does remain for man himself to do. He must exercise faith in committing himself—spirit, soul and body—into union with the Lord Jesus. That is to say, he must reckon the death of the Lord Jesus as his own death and the resurrection of the Lord Jesus as his own resurrection. This is the meaning of John 3:16: "Whoever believes into (literal) him should not perish but have eternal life." The sinner must exercise faith and a believing into the Lord Jesus. By so doing, he is united with Him in His death and resurrection and receives eternal life (John 17:3)—which is spiritual life—unto regeneration.

Let us be careful not to separate into distinct matters the death of the Lord Jesus as our substitute and our death with Him. Those who stress mental understanding will surely so do, but in spiritual life these two are inseparable. Substitutionary death and co-death should be distinguished but never separated. If one believes in the death of the Lord Jesus as his substitute he already has been united with the Lord Jesus in His death (Romans 6:2). For me to believe in the substitutionary work of the Lord Jesus is to believe that I already have been punished in the Lord Jesus. The penalty of my sin is death; yet the Lord Jesus suffered death for me; therefore I have died in Him. There can be no salvation otherwise. To say that He died for me is to say that I already have been penalized and have died in Him. Everyone who believes in this fact shall experience its reality.

Day 5–Morning

Overlooking the Small Karoo area

There is therefore now no condemnation to them that are in Christ Jesus.

Romans 8:1

No Condemnation

Taken from the book: **The Spiritual Man, Vol. I**

Now our sinful humanity has been judged completely because it was judged in the sinless humanity of the Lord Jesus. In Him, holy humanity has won its victory. Whatever judgment should come upon the body, soul and spirit of sinners has been poured upon Him. He is our representative. By faith we are joined to Him. His death is reckoned as our death, and His judgment as our judgment. Our spirit, soul and body have altogether been judged and penalized in Him. It would not be any different had we been punished in person. "There is therefore now no condemnation for those who are in Christ Jesus" (Romans 8:1).

This is what He has accomplished for us and such is now our standing before God. "For he who has died is freed from sin" (Romans 6:7). Positionally we already have died in the Lord Jesus; it only awaits the Holy Spirit to translate this fact into our experience. The cross is where the sinner—spirit, soul and body—is altogether judged. It is through the death and resurrection of the Lord that the Holy Spirit of God is able to impart God's nature to us. The cross bears the sinner's judgment, proclaims the sinner's worthlessness, crucifies the sinner, and releases the life of the Lord Jesus. Henceforth anyone who accepts the cross shall be born anew by the Holy Spirit and receive the life of the Lord Jesus.

Day 5–Evening

Cape of Good Hope Evening Beach Beauty

And as Moses lifted up the serpent in the wilderness, even so must the Son of man be lifted up; that whosoever believeth may in him have eternal life.

John 3:14-15

United with Him

Taken from the book: **The Spiritual Man, Vol. I**

In believing, one is united with the Lord. To be united with Him means to experience everything He has experienced. In John 3 our Lord informs us how we are united with Him. It is by our being united with Him in His crucifixion and death (vv.14-15). Every believer at least positionally has been united with the Lord in His death, but obviously "if we have been united with him in a death like his, we shall certainly be united with him in a resurrection like his" (Romans 6:5). Hence he who believes in the death of the Lord Jesus as his substitute is likewise positionally raised up with Christ. Though he may not yet fully experience the meaning of the death of the Lord Jesus, God nevertheless has made him alive together with Christ and he has obtained a new life in the resurrection power of the Lord Jesus. This is new birth.

We should beware lest we insist that a man is not born anew unless he has experienced death and resurrection with the Lord. The Scriptures deem anyone who believes in the Lord Jesus as already regenerated. "All who received him, who believed in his name ... were ... born of God" (John 1:12-13). Let it be understood that to be raised together with the Lord is not an experience antecedent to the new birth. Our regeneration is our union with the Lord in His resurrection as well as in His death. His death has concluded our sinful walk, and His resurrection has given us a new life and initiated us into the life of a Christian.

Day 6–Morning

The Cape of Storms, Table Bay with Robin Island in the background

Blessed be the God and Father of our Lord Jesus Christ, who according to his great mercy begat us again unto a living hope by the resurrection of Jesus Christ from the dead.

I Peter 1:3

Position vs. Experience

Taken from the book: **The Spiritual Man, Vol. I**

The Apostle assures us that "we have been born anew to a living hope through the resurrection of Jesus Christ from the dead" (I Peter 1:3). He indicates that every born-again Christian has been resurrected already with the Lord. However, the Apostle Paul in Philippians still urges us to experience "the power of His resurrection" (3:10). Many Christians have been born anew and been thus raised with the Lord, even though they are lacking in the manifestation of resurrection power.

Do not confuse, then, position with experience. At the time one believes in the Lord Jesus he may be most weak and ignorant; he is nonetheless placed by God in the perfect position of being considered dead, raised and ascended with the Lord. He who is accepted in Christ is as acceptable as Christ. This is position. And his position is: all that Christ has experienced is his. And position causes him to experience new birth, because it hinges not on how deep he has known experimentally the death, resurrection and ascension of the Lord Jesus, but on whether he has believed in Him. Even if experimentally a believer is totally ignorant of the resurrection power of Christ (Philippians 3:10), he has been made alive together with Christ, raised up with Him and seated with Him in the heavenly places (Ephesians 2:5-6).

Day 6–Evening

Pearly Beach, near the most southern tip of Africa

For the wages of sin is death; but the free gift of God
is eternal life in Christ Jesus our Lord.

Romans 6:23

Salvation and Reward (1)

Taken from the book: **Aids to "Revelation"**

The book of Revelation is a book of righteousness. Yet for us to appreciate its righteous effects, we need to distinguish salvation from reward. The word of God presents a clear distinction between these two. What God has parted, let not men join together. Let us consider this matter carefully and see the contrast between them.

Salvation is that which is given freely. It is not earned by means of man's works. For it is God who gives grace to us, and not on the basis of our merit.

"Ho, every one that thirsteth [points to the sinner], come ye to the waters [points to God's salvation], and he that hath no money [points to works or righteous deeds]; come ye, buy, and eat [means all sinners may believe and be saved]; yea, come, buy wine and milk [means the joy of salvation] without money and without price [points to the fact that there is no need of good deeds, since it does not depend on one's goodness]" (Isaiah 55:1).

Through these verses which have been quoted and many other Scripture passages not quoted, it is proven beyond any doubt that we receive our salvation freely and not by our works or righteous acts; we are saved by the grace of God, the free gift of God. All we do is to believe. For the work of salvation is wholly done for us by the Lord Jesus. His death on the cross has accomplished our salvation. For us now to be saved and to gain eternal life, there is no need for us to perform more works or to add more merits but simply to believe and receive. This is because none of our good works is acceptable to God. Throughout the entire New Testament there are about 150 instances of such sayings as these: believe and be saved, believe and have eternal life, believe and be justified. Just as soon as we believe, we are saved, receive eternal life, and are justified. This is all freely given: "... the witness is this, that God gave unto us eternal life, and this life is in his Son. He that hath the Son hath the life; he that hath not the Son of God hath not the life" (I John 5:11-12). All who accept the Lord Jesus as Savior by faith have eternal life according to the word of God. Truly, "he that believeth on the Son hath eternal life" (John 3:36). Believe and you have!

Day 7–Morning

Western shoreline of the Cape Peninsula with Kommetjie town in the distance

Whatsoever ye do, work heartily, as unto the Lord, and not unto men; knowing that from the Lord ye shall receive the recompense of the inheritance: ye serve the Lord Christ.

Colossians 3:23-24

Salvation and Reward (2)

Taken from the book: **Aids to "Revelation"**

Reward, though, is a different matter. It is not something freely received; it must be obtained through good works. It is given according to the works of each saint. Let us look at the following Scriptures.

"My reward is with me, to render to each man according as his work is" (Revelation 22:12). Note that this word is spoken to the Church (see v.16).

"Each shall receive his own reward according to his own labor" (I Corinthians 3:8). "Now to him that worketh, the reward is not reckoned as of grace" (Romans 4:4).

There are many more Scriptures which could be quoted, but these above are sufficient to prove that reward is not freely received. According to the teaching of the Bible, reward is added to the believer's good works. As insignificant as is a cup of cold water (Matthew 10:42), or as hidden as is the counsel of the heart (I Corinthians 4:5) or as humble as is one's service (Mark 10:43) or as unknown as is the suffering for the Lord's sake (Luke 6:22) — all such deeds or attitudes may still have the opportunity of being rewarded (cf. Luke 6:23).

According to the Bible, the goal which is set before a person is twofold: when we are yet sinners, our goal is salvation; after we are saved and become believers our goal is reward. For salvation is provided for sinners, whereas reward is provided for believers. Men ought to receive salvation first and then pursue after reward. The perishing should receive salvation; and the saved should win reward. By reading I Corinthians 9:24-27 and Philippians 3:12-14, we can readily see that some believers fail to obtain reward. For in these two passages, Paul is talking about reward and not about salvation. He well knows that he is saved. In his other epistles, he frequently expresses himself as one who has received grace. But in these two passages, he tells us of what he is seeking after having been saved and that is, reward. At this moment he dare not say for sure that he has achieved the reward, he instead is still pursuing. Sinners ought to seek for salvation, while believers ought to seek after reward.

Day 7–Evening

Fishermen leaving in the early morning golden rays on the most southern waters of Africa

Know ye not that they that run in a race run all, but one receiveth the prize? Even so run; that ye may attain.

I Corinthians 9:24

Salvation and Reward (3)

Taken from the book: **Aids to "Revelation"**

God is willing to save an undeserving sinner, but He will not reward an undeserving believer. Before anyone believes in the Lord, if he is willing to acknowledge himself as a sinner, come to the Lord Jesus and believe in His substitutionary death on the cross, he is saved and eternal blessing is guaranteed to him. But according to the Scriptures, after he is saved he is placed by God on the race course of life that he may run. If he wins, he shall be rewarded. If he loses, he will not be rewarded. Yet he will not lose eternal life because of his defeat. For salvation is eternal. Here we find the most balanced teaching, the perfect truth. Unfortunately, many people only know salvation. They are content with merely being saved and do not care about the reward.

How sad that people have mixed up salvation with reward. They reckon salvation is most difficult, requiring their supreme efforts of self-discipline to attain it. But this is not the teaching of the Bible. The Scriptures consider salvation to be that which is most easy to come by, for the Lord Jesus by His own initiative has already accomplished everything for us. But the Scriptures regard reward as that which is somewhat harder to obtain because it depends upon the works which we by our initiative accomplish through Christ.

Let us illustrate the matter in this way. Suppose a certain rich man opens a free school. All who attend are free from all charges since this rich man pays for all their expenses. But those who achieve excellence in learning shall receive a special reward. Accordingly, salvation can be likened to entering this free school. All who are willing to come to the Lord Jesus are saved because He himself has paid the cost of salvation. It is very easy to become a student in this free school since it costs nothing. It is enough just to come. In like manner, then, salvation is most easy. One need not do anything except believe. But for one who is now enrolled as a student, to obtain the reward is not that easy; he must work hard. Similarly, it is not so easy for a believer to win the divine reward; he must have good works.

Day 8–Morning

The lonely road through the Gamkaskloof Ravine in the Great Black Mountains down to "The Hell"

If we walk in the light, as he is in the light, we have fellowship one with another, and the blood of Jesus his Son cleanseth us from all sin.

I John 1:7

If Any Man Sin (1)

Taken from the book: **Not I But Christ**

One who has been saved and who afterward sinned again may be greatly distressed by it... They say: I know the Lord has forgiven all my sins, that I am already saved and totally forgiven. But since I have been saved, I have again committed many sins. I am deeply troubled by these sins. What can I do about them?

I hope you have understood that all the sins which you may commit after you are saved are included in the redemption of the Lord Jesus—even though you do not feel forgiven...

By His death on the cross, the Lord Jesus cleansed and redeemed us from all our sins. At the time we came to Him, the Holy Spirit enlightened us and showed us our sins. But what the Holy Spirit showed us was not as comprehensive as what the Lord did on the cross. The difference is worth noticing. Even as the sin-offering in Leviticus 16 included every sin, so also the Lord Jesus on the cross bore all of our sins. His redemption covered every sin that you could possibly commit in your lifetime. Indeed, when He died on the cross, He bore all the sins of your life.

However, when the Holy Spirit inspires us to believe in the Lord, He can only move us to repent of our past sins, not of all the sins of our life. The Holy Spirit's conviction is based on the sins we have already committed, not the sins we have not yet committed! Therefore, on the day we are saved, we are convicted by the light of the Holy Spirit of far fewer sins than those our Lord bore on the cross for us. What the Lord Jesus dealt with on the cross is entirely inclusive; but what I am convicted of by the Holy Spirit and receive forgiveness for, refers only to those sins which I have committed up to the day that I first trust in the Lord...

All sins of the past, all those committed before the day of our salvation no matter what our age at that time, are assuredly forgiven. But we should know that the sins forgiven us then are fewer than the sins which the Lord has actually borne for us. We know the Lord's grace only according to our personal experience of sinning. The Lord, however, has borne all our sins according to His full knowledge of us—that is, all the sins which we will ever commit...

Day 8–Evening

Evening Beauty on the slopes of the Great Black Mountains

If we confess our sins, he is faithful and righteous to forgive us our sins, and to cleanse us from all unrighteousness.

I John 1:9

If Any Man Sin (2)

Taken from the book: **Not I But Christ**

If we know we have sinned and also confess it, God will forgive our sins and cleanse us from all unrighteousness. He is faithful to His own Word and righteous toward His own work, faithful to His own promise and righteous toward the redemptive work of His Son on the cross. He cannot but forgive for He has said it; He must forgive because of the work of redemption. Due to His faithfulness and righteousness, He will forgive us our sins and cleanse us from all unrighteousness (I John 1:9) ...

"My little children, these things write I unto you that ye may not sin. And if any man sin, we have an Advocate with the Father, Jesus Christ the righteous" (I John 2:1). "These things" refers back to the words in chapter 1:7-10; there God depicts in principle our various conditions before Him due to our sins. Because of the blood of Jesus His Son, God forgives us our sins. Owing to His faithfulness and righteousness, He forgives and cleanses all our unrighteousness. No matter what kinds of sins we have committed, they all are forgiven...

When He says "all," no doubt He means "all." Do not change His Word. He forgives not only our sins of the past but all of our sins—sins that we are conscious of as well as those of which we are unaware. We go away with a perfect and complete forgiveness... When we see the Lord's great forgiveness to us, far from becoming careless, we rather are constrained not to sin.

What follows is something quite specific. The sins already mentioned are more general in nature and the forgiveness experienced is also general in principle. But what about the sins committed after we have believed in the Lord? What specific forgiveness is there? "And if any man sin"—this refers to a child of God—"we have an Advocate with the Father, Jesus Christ the righteous." "With the Father" shows that it is a family affair. We are counted among the children of God; we belong to the family. We have an advocate with the Father, even Jesus Christ the righteous, who is the propitiation for our sins. Because He became the propitiation for our sins in His death, He is now our advocate with the Father.

Day 9–Morning

Hout Bay Harbor, Cape Peninsula

My little children, these things write I unto you that ye may not sin. And if any man sin, we have an Advocate with the Father, Jesus Christ the righteous.

I John 2:1

If Any Man Sin (3)

Taken from the book: **Not I But Christ**

If a Christian should sin, he has an advocate with the Father. There is a Father-son relationship if the one who sins is a believer. The word advocate in the Greek is parakletos which means "called to one's side." It has two different usages: in civil use it means one who stands by and is ever ready to help; in legal use it means a counselor or attorney, one who takes full responsibility for the case. Our Lord took us in when we first came to His cross. How did He assume our case? By being "the propitiation for our sins and not for ours only, but also for the whole world" (I John 2:2). There is no need for a new cross, for the redemptive work of the cross is eternally efficacious.

New believers should clearly be exhorted not to sin. They ought not to sin and it is actually possible for them not to sin. But if they should unfortunately sin, let them remember that the blood of the Lord Jesus can still cleanse them from all their sins. He is their champion; He is the righteous One. The very fact that He is now with the Father guarantees the forgiveness of their sins.

Since this is so, do not linger in the shame of sin... If any man sin, the first thing to do is to go to God and confess, "I have sinned." This is judging oneself, calling sin by its right name. "If we confess our sins, He is faithful and righteous to forgive us our sins, and to cleanse us from all unrighteousness." If you do this, you will then see that God forgives you and that your fellowship with Him is immediately restored. ... If a child of God should sin and continue in that sin without confession, he yet remains God's child and God is still his Father. Nevertheless, his fellowship with God will be lost. ...

There is only one way to be restored. I must go to God and confess my sin. I believe that the Lord Jesus is my advocate and has taken care of all my sins. So here I am before God, humbly acknowledging my failure. I look to the Lord that hereafter I may not be so arrogant and careless. I have learned how prone I am to fall. I am no better than others. So I pray that God may be merciful to me, that I may continue on with the Lord step by step. Praise God, we do have an advocate with Him, One who does come alongside.

Day 9–Evening

Sweetwater Beach, viewing the Atlantic Ocean

Blessed be the God and Father of our Lord Jesus Christ, who hath blessed us with every spiritual blessing in the heavenly places in Christ.

Ephesians 1:3

Boundless Possibility for Growth

Taken from the book: **The Spiritual Man, Vol. I**

A life relationship is established with God in new birth. It resembles the old birth of the flesh in that it is once and for all. Once a man is born of God he can never be treated by God as not having been so born of Him. However endless eternity may be, this relationship and this position cannot be annulled. This is because what a believer receives at new birth is not contingent upon a progressive, spiritual and holy pursuit after he believes but is the pure gift of God. What God bestows is eternal life. No possibility exists for this life and position to be abrogated.

Receiving God's life in new birth is the starting point of a Christian walk, the minimum for a believer. Those who have not yet believed on the death of the Lord Jesus and received supernatural life (which they cannot possess naturally), are deemed in the sight of God to be dead, no matter how religious, moral, learned or zealous they may be. Those who do not have God's life are dead.

For those who are born anew, there is great potentiality for spiritual growth. Regeneration is the obvious first step in spiritual development. Though the life received is perfect, it waits to be matured. At the moment of new birth life cannot be full-grown. It is like a fruit newly formed: the life is perfect but it is still unripe. There is therefore boundless possibility for growth. The Holy Spirit is able to bring the person into complete victory over body and soul.

Day 10–Morning

One of the Cape of Storms' Lighthouses

Because Christ also suffered for sins once, the righteous for the unrighteous, that he might bring us to God; being put to death in the flesh, but made alive in the spirit.

I Peter 3:18

Resurrection Life

Taken from the book: **The Spirit of Wisdom and Revelation**

"And I was dead, and behold, I am alive for evermore" (Revelation 1:18).

"And I was dead"—Our Lord did in fact once become dead. On the one hand He died as a substitute for sinners. It was a case of "the righteous [dying] for the unrighteous" (I Peter 3:18). On the other hand, through His death He released His life. How marvelous is this death! "And, behold, I am alive for evermore"—Christ has risen from the dead. Innumerable people encounter death and die. Yet none has ever come back; no one by his own power has ever been resurrected. Indeed, during these thousands of years of human history millions and billions of people have passed away. "To go and not to return" seems to have been the unchanging rule since we have not seen any ever come back. Yet God allowed our Lord Jesus to die that through death He might prove His victory over death. He did become dead, but now He is alive forever. How great is this declaration: "I am alive for evermore"!

At the time of Pentecost the apostle Peter unequivocally declared: "[Jesus] God raised up, having loosed the pangs of death: because it was not possible that he should be holden of it" (Acts 2:24). Death could not hold Him because death has no power to hold Him. The resurrection life can endure death. Though dead, now resurrected—this very fact of history proves how Christ's life can endure death and is able to pass through death. Many encounter something unpleasant and immediately feel as though they are meeting up with death. But this resurrection life of the Lord Jesus is not afraid to die. By passing through death it proves its power to outlive death. Resurrection life is that which can pass through death and still live. Whatever passes through death but is finished is not resurrection life.

Day 10–Evening

A view of Sea Point's golden evening glitter from Signal Hill

And without faith it is impossible to be well-pleasing unto him; for he that cometh to God must believe that he is, and that he is a rewarder of them that seek after him.

Hebrews 11:6

Faith

Taken from the book: **A Balanced Christian Life**

Faith is a principle of our Christian walk. Faith is governed by two rules that are represented by a gate and a way. All who are familiar with spiritual experience know that faith is composed of "believe" and "trust." There is a difference between the act of faith and the attitude of faith. To believe once and for all is what we call passing through a crisis, but to trust continuously afterwards is what we call making progress. Exercising a single-minded act of faith is entering the gate, but maintaining an attitude of faith thereafter is walking in the way. In order for a Christian to truly believe in God in a particular matter, he must with singleness of heart first exercise an act of faith by which he truly believes in God before he can ever walk the way of faith. In entering the gate of faith he crosses a threshold of doubt, and thus with single-heartedness he receives from God a promise. This is passing through the gate or going through a crisis. Please remember that believers must first enter through such a gate of faith, and then they may advance in the walk of faith by maintaining an attitude of faith. Many people speculate that they can trust God by maintaining an attitude of faith without ever crossing the threshold of faith by means of a single-minded act of faith. They do not know that without entering the gate there is absolutely no possibility of their walking in the way... It is imperative that there be a clear break with the past and a definite acceptance of the testimony of God. This is entering the gate; otherwise, there can never be any spiritual advancement...

Let all of us remember that if we expect to walk in the way of obedience, we must pass through the crisis of consecration; ... we will make no spiritual progress without consecration. It is imperative that we be disarmed by God. We should not dream of walking in the way of obedience if we have never walked through the gate of obedience. When we are redeemed, we no doubt belong to God. But beginning from the moment of our consecration we shall experience that we really do belong to Him.

Day 11–Morning

At the foot of Lion's Head, Capetown

I beseech you therefore, brethren, by the mercies of God, to present your bodies a living sacrifice, holy, acceptable to God, which is your spiritual service.

Romans 12:1

Consecration

Taken from the book: **The Life That Wins**

We ought to know the purpose of God in creating us and in redeeming us. He wishes for us to manifest the life of His Son and share in His Son's glory. Even before the foundation of the world, God has purposed one purpose, which is to say, that He wants to have many sons just as He has the only begotten Son. And thus it states in Romans 8:29: "whom he foreknew, he also foreordained to be conformed to the image of his Son, that he might be the firstborn among many brethren."...

This is the eternal purpose of God. He purchases and redeems us that He may possess us. Yet God uses two means to possess us: one is on His side, the other is on our side. On His side, God sent His Son to die for us, to buy us back. According to the right of purchase, we are His bondslaves. Thank the Lord, He has bought us. God once said to Abraham, "He that is born in the house, and he that is bought with money, must needs be circumcised" (Genesis 17:13). Hallelujah, we are not only born of God we are also bought by Him. We are bought by God and thus belong to Him, yet He sets us free. Although according to the right of redemption we belong to God, He nonetheless will not force us into service. He will let us go if we desire to serve mammon, the world, the belly, or other idols. For the moment God is inactive: He is waiting for us to move: till one day we say on our side: "O God, I am Your bondslave not only because You have bought me, but also because I will gladly serve You."

A verse in Romans 6 unveils a most precious principle concerning consecration. We become God's bondslaves not only for the reason that He has bought us, but also for the reason "that to whom ye present yourselves as servants unto obedience, his servants ye are whom ye obey" (v.16a). Here, then, are the two means by which God possesses us. On the one side, we are His bondslaves because He has bought us; on the other side, we willingly and gladly present ourselves to Him as His bondslaves. As regards law, we become God's bondslaves on the day He purchased and redeemed us. As regards experience, we become His bondslaves on the day we offer up ourselves to Him.

Day 11—Evening

Table Mountain and Capetown city from Blueberg Beach

Now the just shall live by faith: but if any man draw back, my soul shall have no pleasure in him.

Hebrews 10:38 KJV

Faith Is Rest (1)

Taken from the book: **The Spirit of Judgment**

Now it is just here that this issue of faith enters into the picture. Faith is composed of two basic principles: (1) To cease from man's own work, and (2) to wait for God to work. Ordinarily we consider faith as trusting, depending and waiting for God to work; not realizing that there is the prerequisite of ceasing our own work first. To cease from man's own work is reckoned as a work of faith. Waiting for God to work happens in the believer's heart, hence it is invisible; but ceasing from one's own work is external, therefore it may sometimes be seen. The greater work of faith is manifested in the believer ceasing from his own work rather than in waiting for God to work for him. The importance of such a step cannot be overemphasized. For God is never willing to mix His own work in with the work of man's flesh. What God requires of the believer is to cease from all that is of his own self, including his idea and strength. No doubt God is pleased to be trusted and relied upon by the believer. But how is such faith in God expressed? By being still and completely resting from one's self. This is the first step in the work of faith. ...

See how wise is our God! For if faith were something we ourselves had and it came out from us, why, we would then become its master. Whenever we wanted to do a particular thing, we would only need to believe and we would have God to work it out for us. But this is not so. Faith is something given by God. Before He gives us faith, we just cannot believe.

Day 12–Morning

Scarborough, Cape Peninsula

For by grace have ye been saved through faith; and that not of yourselves, it is the gift of God; not of works, that no man should glory. For we are his workmanship, created in Christ Jesus for good works, which God afore prepared that we should walk in them.

Ephesians 2:8-10

Faith Is Rest (2)

Taken from the book: **The Spirit of Judgment**

Many of us Christians share in the experience of frequently finding no way to enter into rest because we simply are unable to manufacture faith. Then suddenly God gives faith (sometimes it comes through one or two scripture passages; sometimes it comes after prayer when we know intuitively the will of God), and our heart immediately calms down and enters into rest, as if a kind of assurance has been given to us that God will do the work. Such faith comes naturally without the need of struggling, anxiety, and exercise. As soon as God grants faith, the believer instantly exhibits the work of faith, which is rest without worrying. Whatever is humanly manufactured is not faith, and therefore does not give rest.

A word of cautionary discernment is necessary at this point. For what has been mentioned above does not mean that now we have no other responsibility but to wait for faith to come. Faith actually may be divided into two kinds: the special and the ordinary. Special faith is given to us by God concerning some particular matter, thus enabling us to believe that God will accomplish it for us. Such special faith does not happen on every occasion. Ordinary faith is the faith which an experienced believer always has towards God. It is not directed at a particular matter, but rather towards all matters. Such faith assumes the believing attitude that whatever God does is right. Failure or success is all within the perfect will of God. Although we have special faith only occasionally, we ought to have ordinary faith towards all things which come our way, believing our God can do no wrong, trusting that everything is in His hands, and acknowledging He knows what is best for us, whether suffering or success. We should have this ordinary faith at all times. Even when special things happen, we must not lose this kind of faith.

Day 12–Evening

A peaceful evening at Walker Bay

Verily, verily, I say unto you, Except a grain of wheat fall into the earth and die, it abideth by itself alone; but if it die, it beareth much fruit.

John 12:24

Redemption's Work

Taken from the book: **God's Plan and the Overcomers**

The redemption of Christ solves the problem of Satan's rebellion. It is not just the cross of Christ that overcomes Satan; it is His blood. Satan well knew that if he could inject his poison into the first married pair, this poison would propagate itself in all who would be born by them. Consequently, Satan and our forefathers committed spiritual fornication by which the lying poison of sin entered the soul of our forefathers. Since the soul life is in the blood (see Leviticus 17:11 mg.), therefore this sinful human life has been reproduced throughout the generations ("he made of one blood every nation of men"—Acts 17:26 Stephens' Greek Text, 1550). The sinful poison injected into the first couple has flowed into our life through the blood. The blood of Christ contains no poison. It is the precious blood and is incorruptible. On the cross He bore the sins of many and poured out all His blood in death. When Christ was raised from the dead He had no blood. After His resurrection He has bones and flesh but no blood, "because he poured out his soul unto death" (Isaiah 53:12). In Christ our blood has already been poured out. Hence Satan has no more ground of operation in our lives. The blood of Christ has destroyed and finished Satan and all who are his.

The redemption of Christ also resolves the problem of the sin of man. Our sins require the death of Christ. His substitutionary death dismisses our criminal case before God. His representative death delivers us from the dominion of sin.

Day 13–Morning

Overlooking the Valley of Desolation

Looking for the blessed hope and appearing of the glory of the great God and our Saviour Jesus Christ; who gave himself for us, that he might redeem us from all iniquity, and purify unto himself a people for his own possession, zealous of good works. Titus 2:13-14

Redemption's Purpose

Taken from the book: **God's Plan and the Overcomers**

The purpose of the redemption of Christ is to make us a people for His own possession (Titus 2:14) that we might be a living sacrifice to Him (Romans 12:1): living and dying for Him (Romans 14:7-9, II Corinthians 5:15) and serving as the Temple of the Holy Spirit to glorify God (I Corinthians 6:19, 20)—so that Christ might be magnified in us whether by life or by death, because for us to live is Christ (Philippians 1:20,21). The aim of redemption is to let Christ have the preeminence in all things. In order to have this first place in all things, Christ must first have the preeminence in us. And why? Because we are the firstfruits of all creation (cf. James 1:18). After we are in subjection to Christ, all other things will follow in subjection. The cross works in our lives to enable God to realize this aim in us. Is it not the cross that decreases us and increases Christ? The cross seeks out for Christ the place of preeminence. God uses the cross, which in turn works through circumstances to dig deeply into our lives so as to make us know Christ and be filled with Him for the sake of obtaining for Him the preeminence in us. The redemption of Christ is to realize God's plan which was laid before the foundation of the world so that Christ might have the first place in all things. How we need to disregard our personal gain or loss and to regard God's foreordained will in order for Christ to have the preeminence in all things. As we see the Messiah, we will cast away the waterpot in our hand! (see John 4) When we see Christ we will forsake all things!

Day 13–Evening

Misty Morning in the Great Karoo

For I know that in me, that is, in my flesh, dwelleth no good thing: for to will is present with me, but to do that which is good is not. For the good which I would I do not: but the evil which I would not, that I practise.

Romans 7:18-19

The Failure of the Self (1)

Taken from the books: **Spiritual Knowledge & The Messenger of the Cross**

Many Christians carelessly let difficulties or problems pass by without receiving dealings from God. They do not know why He sends them these difficulties. These people may read the Bible daily and seem to possess some knowledge and light, yet they are ignorant of the mind of God. Their knowledge is clearly insufficient. For this cause, beloved, we must deal with God and receive dealings from God; and then shall we truly know Him...

To know one's self is to be deprived of glory; to deny one's self is to make oneself suffer. So that in reality a believer is not too eager to know himself and therefore he does not know himself that well; indeed, he will ignorantly deem himself as trustworthy. Now because of the believer's unwillingness to have such self-knowledge, the Holy Spirit is not able to reveal to him his true character in the sight of God. As a result, the Lord is forced to use some painful means to make a believer know himself. And the means most frequently used is to let the believer fail. ...

Although the Lord hates "self" so much, the attitude of believers towards it is quite different. They delight in depending on self, cherishing self, and glorying in self. They are ignorant of their true self; and neither do they know how unclean and corrupt and weak the self is in God's eyes... If in such a situation they should make much progress, experiencing an increasing number of successes and victories, their self life will be nourished and grow bigger and it will thus become harder to deny. Each time they do a good deed, they drift a step further from the life of God. A little more power of their own means a little more distance away from the Holy Spirit. More success results in more glory to self, hence prolonging the evil life of self. ...

God has no other aim than to lead you to the end of yourself that you may know yourself. This is thus the explanation for why, when sometimes you have struggled to overcome, you nevertheless have failed.

Day 14–Morning

Karoo National Reserve

Wretched man that I am! who shall deliver me out of the body of this death? I thank God through Jesus Christ our Lord.

Romans 7:24-25a

The Failure of the Self (2)

Taken from the book: **The Messenger of the Cross**

Oh how you cried, you strove, you fought, you pursued, you prayed, you worked and labored, you employed all kinds of means to overcome sin and reach holiness; yet you ended up in defeat. Although at times you did experience a little victory, such victory was only temporary. You tried your best to sustain it, but it flew away like a bird. You concluded that you were worse than all, and therefore you could not gain the victory. Such experiences find their meaning in the fact that God was leading you to know your own self. It is not because you were too corrupt to gain a victory; rather, it was because you were not corrupt enough in your own eyes to win the victory. You ought to recognize that it is you yourself who cried, it was you who struggled and fought, it was you yourself who prayed and pursued, that it was you who worked and labored. You were the one active, and it was all for your own self....

How many tears are shed today not for the sake of sin, but for the sake of "self" that is incapable of reaching the expected goodness of a believer. Much seeking, prayers and faith appear to be directed towards God, yet within all these endeavors is most likely the anticipation of self-good. And hence God permits you to be defeated again and again so that you may see finally the utter corruption of the flesh. And once your weakness is proven by such defeats, it is hoped by God that you may know your true self, forsake it and turn to trust in Him.

Each defeat ought to give you a little more knowledge of yourself. Each failure should show you a little more of your weakness. Each sin should make you expect less of yourself and make you more willing to forsake your self. ...

God will let a believer fail until he willingly acknowledges, "I am sold under sin! There is no good in me!" Not till then will he know that except a power comes from outside, he is hopeless and helpless. But then he will cry out: "Wretched man that I am! Who shall deliver me?" (Romans 7:24) When he really perceives how corrupt he is, he will then know and acknowledge that unless Christ rescues him he cannot overcome sin.

Day 14–Evening

Descending into the Small Karoo out of the Great Black Mountains on the dirt road

For he that is dead is freed from sin.

Romans 6:7 KJV

In Adam

Taken from the book: **Gleanings In the Fields of Boaz**

Romans 5 shows us we are in Adam; Romans 6 tells us we are in Christ. Romans 7 exposes the fact of how we yet live in the flesh, whereas Romans 8 educates us about how to live in the Spirit. Whenever we live in the flesh, everything we get from Adam is there. But if we live in the Spirit, then all that is in Christ becomes ours. Hence we need revelation as to how we are in Christ and to believe it. Then we must yield to the Holy Spirit and obey Him in order to live according to the Spirit and experience all that is in Christ. Many Christians, however, fail to realize that they are in Adam. Therefore they see no need of being delivered out of him. They think that after their sins are forgiven, all their problems now lie in their behavior. They do not see that the real issue is in themselves. How many of us reason that if we can only change our habits, ways, thoughts, acts, and so forth, we will be all right. Not so, however; for there must be a complete exchange of life. We must be displaced and replaced with Christ. We must see that whether we win or not, we ourselves are rotten and vile, altogether Adamic.

Fundamentally speaking, we share Adam's very life. We are born of Adam. We are by nature Adamic. How does God treat us little Adams? "He that hath died is justified [or, released, mg.] from sin" (Romans 6:7). How did we get into Adam in the first place? Whose responsibility is it that we are in Adam? Whose fault and by whose work do we obtain this sinful nature of Adam? We can trace all this back to one person, Adam himself. All was done by Adam, not by us individually. In the same way, we get free of Adam and receive a new life with a new nature through another Person and His work.

Day 15–Morning

An Atlantic Ocean Sunset from Lion's Head, Capetown

I am the vine, ye are the branches: He that abideth in me, and I in him, the same beareth much fruit: for apart from me ye can do nothing.

John 15:5

In Christ

Taken from the book: **Gleanings In the Fields of Boaz**

When Adam ate the forbidden fruit in the Garden of Eden, we were there in the loins of Adam. We too ate of it and failed God. We disobeyed God and sinned against Him. The entity and the solidarity of the human race come to the fore here. Just so is it also with our righteousness received from Christ and our being in Christ: "of him [God] are ye in Christ Jesus" (I Corinthians 1:30). Because God has put us in Christ, all which God has done in Christ, all which He has given to Christ—even all the work and nature of Christ—become ours. If we look within ourselves, we cannot see how we were in Adam; therefore we cannot believe it. Likewise, if we look within ourselves, we cannot see how we are in Christ. Accordingly, we must look away from ourselves and look off to Christ. We must see ourselves in Christ there at Calvary. For by looking within ourselves, we will never believe that we have been crucified and have died. All we see will be our sins, defeats and failure. But if we look at Christ and see ourselves in Him, we will know that we have died in spite of what we may see within ourselves or what our life experiences tell us. Hence it all depends on whether or not we have seen this glorious fact, whether or not our eyes have been opened to see ourselves being in Christ.

It is not that we are "identified" with Christ, but that we actually are "included" in Christ. This requires revelation. With revelation everything will change. The word does not say, "Abide into Christ." It says, "Abide in Christ." We are already there in Christ. Do not get out. Satan tries to get us to look at our life, experiences and defeats in order to say to us that we are not in Christ. We should never say a word or entertain a thought which even approaches our not being in Christ. We must hold unwaveringly, absolutely and tenaciously to the glorious reality that we are in Christ at all times.

Day 15–Evening

One of the tips of the Great Black Mountains

Knowing this, that our old man was crucified with him, that the body of sin might be done away, that so we should no longer be in bondage to sin.

Romans 6:6

Our Old Man Is Crucified

Taken from the book: **Back to the Cross**

This is a co-crucifixion, not a single crucifixion. Apart from the Lord, we can do nothing. To crucify self with our own power is a myth. It can never be done. Unless we have died in the Lords death, we will never die. Christ alone in His death brought the old creation and all to the cross. It is foolish and futile to set up another way other than Christ or attempt another plan other than His. Hence, there is nothing left for us to do but to confess that what Christ has accomplished is ours and to ask the Holy Spirit to apply the work of the cross in us.

Simply come to God, deny self and surrender all. Let us deliver our self life, with all that it contains, to the death of Christ's cross by the Spirit of the Lord. We ought to say to God: "Hereafter it is no longer I, no longer my delight, idea, interest and prejudice. I deliver all to the cross. From now on, I will live only for Your will. Lord, it is You, not I." We should thus yield to the Lord and deliver our all to death. This, though, does not mean that henceforth our "self" is annihilated. No, self cannot be annihilated, nor should it be annihilated. Self will remain forever. But if that be so, then, why must self be crucified?

Here we need to understand an essential point: the problem before us is one concerning spiritual life. Such a problem lays stress on spiritual experience rather than on literary consistency. Many things might appear contradictory—even beyond reconciliation—in letter; yet, in spiritual life they are quite complementary void of any conflict. The very case before us falls into this category. According to letter, self seems to have died. How, then, is it not annihilated? Do realize that the word "dead" employed here is descriptive of a kind of experimental process. To say the death of self within this context of spiritual life does not suggest that hereafter there is no more self. It says instead that henceforth self will obey God, self will no longer be allowed to sit on the throne—it will be crucified, and all its selfish actions will cease. The self life will no longer be permitted to utilize self. For the self life and its living is now dead. There remains no more self life and its living. What is left is merely its skeleton.

Day 16–Morning

The Arniston Shipwreck at Cape L'Agullus, the most southern tip of Africa

If any man would come after me, let him deny himself, and take up his cross daily, and follow me.

Luke 9:23

Take Up the Cross Daily

Taken from the book: **Back to the Cross**

"If any man would come after me, let him deny himself, and take up his cross daily, and follow me" Luke 9:23.

This verse shows us three things we should do; yet actually, they are not three separate things but a single three-fold matter. The first step is to deny self. To deny means to forsake, to not care, to not be concerned about, to not acknowledge any demand. Denying self means a not letting self rule. This step is a singular action which needs to be taken by specifically believing that "I have been crucified with Christ." In order to protect this step, we must take another and second step, and that is: "take up his cross daily." This shows that once we have willed to deliver self to the cross and not let it rule, we then must daily deny self. So that to "deny self" is a "daily" matter—never to be interrupted. To "deny self" cannot only be a once-and-for-all action. Paul declares, "I die daily" (I Corinthians 15:31). The Lord will give us a cross that we might bear it daily, because self is intensely alert; and Satan, who utilizes self, is untiring. Self is seeking for a chance to be re-enthroned. It will not lightly pass over any conceivable opportunity. Consequently, our taking up the cross daily is most essential.

Here lies the watchfulness required of believers. We ought to daily, nay, hourly, take up the cross that the Lord has given to us. Confess incessantly that the cross of Christ is our cross. Make no provision for self, nor let it have any position. And finally, the third step is to "follow me [the Lord], which is to positively let the Lord be Lord, fully obeying the will of God and giving no opportunity nor possibility for self to renew its effort. All three of these steps or stages are centered upon the cross of Christ—which is to say that all three have it as their source. The first step—to deny self—is negative; the second step—to take up the cross—is negatively positive; and the third step—to follow the Lord—is totally positive.

Day 16–Evening

Wagon House Cliff Cave at Arniston

Even so reckon ye also yourselves to be dead unto sin, but alive unto God in Christ Jesus.

Romans 6:11

Reckon (1)

Taken from the book: **Back to the Cross**

A believer (one who has confessed his sins and has been saved by faith in the Lord Jesus) ought to have well in mind that the crucifying of his old man is not an independent act outside of the Lord Jesus; rather, it is accomplished through union with the Lord Jesus. As Christ died, our old man died with Him, too, for it died in His death. The ignorance of this fact explains the failure of many. Believers tend to use their own power to crucify the old man. Yet however much they may try, that old man is still alive, because it is absolutely impossible for them individually to crucify the old man outside of Christ. Most believers do this through ignorance. They do not know that apart from dying with Christ, there is no other way to put the old man to death. The old man is to be crucified with Christ. ...

"Even so reckon ye also yourselves to be dead unto sin, but alive unto God in Christ Jesus" (Romans 6:11). This word "reckon" is of utmost importance. We all want to "touch" and see if our old man is dead. We always like to "feel" whether our old man is dead or not. Yet, if it depends on our "touch" or "feel", our old man will never die, since he does not die simply because we "touch" or "feel." As a matter of fact, the more we "touch," the livelier will be our old man; the more we "feel", the more present will be our old man. The old man is not crucified by "touch" or "feel"; he is crucified through "reckoning."

What is it to "reckon"? To "reckon" is to exercise faith, to "reckon" is to exercise the judgment as well as the execution of the will. "Reckoning" is totally different from "touching" or "feeling." For these latter are related to the senses; but "reckoning" is in the realm of faith and will. Hence, the way to deal with the old man does not lie in the realm of feeling. To say "I do not feel my old man is dead" is totally wrong. The death of the old man does not depend on whether or not you feel it so; it is determined by whether or not you reckon it so.

Day 17–Morning

Namibian west coast desert road from Aus to Helmeringhausen

Likewise reckon ye also yourselves to be dead indeed unto sin, but alive unto God through Jesus Christ our Lord.

Romans 6:11 KJV

Reckon (2)

Taken from the book: **Back to the Cross**

How do you "reckon"? To reckon yourself as dead to sin is to account yourself as already crucified, that is, to account your old man as already crucified. It is reckoning the cross of the Lord Jesus Christ to be also the cross of your old man. Thus you consider the death of the Lord Jesus to be likewise the death of your old man. Indeed, you deem the time when the Lord Jesus died nineteen hundred years ago as having been as well the exact time of the death of your old man. For the old man having been crucified with Christ is a fact, an accomplished fact. In the eyes of God, the sin factor is already dead; and so, we must reckon ourselves to be dead to this sin factor. In our believing from the heart that God will realize in us what we reckon, and in our deciding with the will that we have died to sin, we shall no longer be bondservants of sin.

This "reckoning" is an attitude as well as an action. An action is taken once, but an attitude is constantly maintained. An action is taken as a timely move against a certain matter; an attitude is maintained as a lasting estimation of that matter. We ought to reckon ourselves as dead to sin. This is to say that we should take a singular action of reckoning ourselves as dead, and then follow through by a permanent attitude of reckoning ourselves as indeed dead to sin. Action commences; attitude continues. We ought once and singularly to reckon before God, believing ourselves to be dead from that day onward. Having taking that action, we then need to affirm it daily with a corresponding attitude—that is to say, with maintaining the belief of our being dead to sin. ...

Here again, though, God's children encounter difficulty. They are troubled by their "forgetting" to reckon. But they have used the wrong faculty. For, reckoning is the judgment of the will, not the consideration of the mind. Whether you overcome or not depends on your attitude of reckoning yourself as dead, not on your memory of reckoning.

Day 17–Evening

On the Road from Solitaire to Walvis Bay, Namibia

Even so reckon ye also yourselves to be dead unto sin, but alive unto God in Christ Jesus.

Romans 6:11

Reckon (3)

Taken from the book: **Back to the Cross**

Through the power of the Holy Spirit and the exercise of your will in maintaining this death attitude, you may consciously or unconsciously possess this attitude, which remains the same whether remembering or forgetting. Naturally, the mind has its place, but it is not necessary for it to affect the will. The will should instead control the mind and cause the latter to help the former in sustaining this attitude.

Let us stand, therefore, on the ground of the cross and let us—daily, hourly, consciously and unconsciously—reckon our old man as dead. This is the secret of overcoming sin and the devil. We know that sin and the devil are closely related. If sin does not reign in us, the devil will have no ground in us.

If believers will understand and accept this aspect of the truth of the cross, apostasy and defeat shall be greatly diminished. Lasting victory is inseparable from constant standing on the ground of the cross.

Nevertheless, even after we take the action and maintain the attitude of reckoning our old man to be dead, the sinful nature in us does not henceforth become annihilated and disappear. For as long as we live in this mortal body, the sinful nature will co-exist with us. To say that our sinful nature can be annihilated in this life is a great heresy. We can deliver the old man to death by the power of the cross of Calvary and render it powerless and withered as though dead, but we cannot annihilate it. Whenever we are careless and unwatchful, whenever we do not stand on the death ground of Calvary, our old man will renew its activities and resume its office. Satan is always looking for an opportunity to reactivate the old man. And as soon as there is a loophole, the old man will recover its original position.

In view of this, we ought to be watchful lest the old man be revived. Is not this most difficult? Indeed, it is hard to the flesh. For this reason, a believer must have the power of the Holy Spirit in letting the cross work in him.

Day 18–Morning

Plattekloof Gorge, Table Mountain, Capetown

For the word of God is living, and active, and sharper than any two-edged sword, and piercing even to the dividing of soul and spirit, of both joints and marrow, and quick to discern the thoughts and intents of the heart. Hebrews 4:12

Discernment

Taken from the book: **The Messenger of the Cross**

What therefore is soulish? Soulish is that which is done by oneself. And what therefore is spiritual? It is that which is done by God. And these two are radically different. A person can do something without any need for waiting upon God and trusting in Him. Such action is fleshly and it is soulish. But if a person cannot speak before God speaks, cannot move except God moves first; if he must look to God, wait and depend on Him—then that person and that action is spiritual. Let us thus ask ourselves if all we do is in the Holy Spirit? This is such an important question. Frequently there is nothing wrong in what we do, nevertheless there is condemnation registered within us when we do it. The reason for this inward sense is not that what we do outwardly is necessarily wrong but because the thing we do is not initiated from God—that is to say, it is not the outcome of the working of the Holy Spirit in us. ...

In spiritual things, self-analysis will not only fail to show us the reality, it will even create spiritual paralysis. Real seeing and understanding comes only from God's illumination. As light shines, we just naturally see. We therefore do not need to ask ourselves questions; all we need to do is to ask God to cause His word to shine in us, for the word of God is living and most effective; it is sharper than any two-edged sword and pierces even to dividing between soul and spirit, between both joints and marrow. As soon as the word of God enters, you can immediately perceive what is soulish from what is spiritual. There is a judgment within you which is sharper than any human judgment. If you make a move, your inward sense tells you that this move is not right or not deep enough, or that it is you who are doing things and you who are trying to influence people. When you see inwardly, you really see. May God have mercy upon us by granting the inner light by which we may distinguish inwardly.

The dividing of soul and spirit is the foundation for a Christian to have discerning power. Yet whether we have this discerning power or not depends on inward illumination and not on outward instruction. [God's] word will give light so that He may show us what in our personal life and work is soulish or what is spiritual.

Day 18–Evening

A Rosey Sunset in the Evening Sky of Table Bay

Let us therefore draw near with boldness unto the throne of grace, that we may receive mercy, and may find grace to help us in time of need.

Hebrews 4:16

Worship Boldly by the Blood

Taken from the book: **From Faith to Faith**

Many have the idea that they may come to God and worship Him because they have good works which are worthy of His praise. They cannot come and worship if they have not behaved themselves but have done things displeasing to God. Yet we need to understand that our conduct, whether good or bad, has no direct relationship to our approaching God: "Having therefore, brethren, boldness to enter into the holy place by the blood of Jesus" (Hebrews 10:19). We are told in this verse that our coming to God is based on nothing else than the blood of the Lord Jesus. Neither good works nor zeal nor spiritual experience qualifies us to approach God. The blood of the Lord Jesus alone enables us to draw near to Him. ...

We know we are different from the children of Israel in worship, since all of us today may enter into the holiest of all and worship God because of the blood; but the children of Israel could not do so. The Old Testament or Covenant presents to us a picture of distance, for the congregation could not do anything by themselves. They could not worship directly. Even the slaying of cattle and sheep had to be done by the priests. They were separated from God; they could not draw near to Him. Not so, though, under the New Testament or Covenant. Each and every believer may come to worship in the holiest place. ...

Romans mentions the blood upon the mercy seat which deals with the one aspect of our sin being atoned for. Hebrews speaks of the blood before the veil which deals with the other aspect, that of drawing near to worship God. For the blood not only forgives and cleanses us of sin, it also leads us to approach God and worship Him. Some may still object and argue that they have not behaved well during the week, and therefore they dare not come to God with boldness. Then let me ask you, When will you be good enough to feel that there is nothing wrong with you so that you may come and worship with boldness? How long will you have to wait for such a day? When will your heart be able to burst forth with hallelujahs? According to your own requirements, you will not be able to worship until after you are raptured! Let us see that our worship is not determined by our works but by our trusting in the blood.

Day 19–Morning

Pongola Mountain Pass Dam, KwaZulu Natal, South Africa

Blessed are the merciful: for they shall obtain mercy.

Matthew 5:7

Forgiveness (1)

Taken from the book: **Gospel Dialogue**

Concerning the forgiveness in the kingdom we may read Matthew 18:21-35 ... Concerning the church God speaks of grace; concerning the kingdom, He speaks of responsibility. As regards the church, we are told what the Lord has done and how He treats us; as regards the kingdom, we are shown how we are trained before God, how we live today, and what will be the judgment in the future. Here in Matthew 18 we are shown our responsibility, for this passage is concerned with the kingdom of heaven—with reigning for a thousand years—and not with the question of eternal salvation. ...

We know that the daily life and work of a Christian on earth will be judged in the future. After the rapture all Christians will stand in judgment before the judgment seat of Christ. This is not to be a judging of the salvation of a Christian but the judging of his fitness for the kingdom and his position in the kingdom. Thus there are two perils in our standing before the judgment seat: first, we may be barred completely from the kingdom; or, second, we may receive a low position in the kingdom if we are allowed to enter. ...

Since judgment is to begin at the house of God (I Peter 4:17), how serious must be this judgment! And if so, who can pass this judgment? How must we expect God to be merciful to us at the judgment seat, for even there we need grace! This is exactly what Matthew 18 is talking about. It is true that God will judge us with absolute justice; nevertheless, there is forgiveness with Him, and His forgiveness is based on our forgiving others today. No matter how people may treat you, if you forgive five or ten persons who sin against you and you always forgive, then in that day God will treat you justly. Because you have forgiven others, it is most just for God to forgive you at the judgment seat. ...

We need to be careful daily about two things: one is to examine ourselves lest we fall into the judgment of God; and the other is, that however much people may owe us, let us be merciful and forgiving so that we may receive God's forgiveness on that day.

Day 19–Evening

Beautiful sighting of Oryx in the Namib Desert, Naukluft

And forgive us our debts, as we also have forgiven our debtors.

Matthew 6:12

Forgiveness (2)

Taken from the book: **Not I But Christ**

The Lord expects you to treat others as He has treated you. Since He does not demand of you according to righteousness, He expects you not to demand righteousness of others. The Lord forgives your debt according to mercy. With what measure He has meted out to you, He wants you to mete out to others. He gives you in good measure, pressed down, shaken together and running over; He wishes you to do likewise. As He treats you, so should you treat your brother. It is exceedingly ugly in the sight of God for the forgiven person to be unforgiving. Nothing can be uglier than for the one who was forgiven to be unforgiving, the one who received mercy to be merciless, and the one who was given grace to be graceless. We must learn before God to treat others as He has treated us. Let us be so humbled by what we have received that we treat others according to the same principle. ...

I believe many of God's children have learned the lesson of forgiveness. Many, though, have forgotten what we should do after someone has sinned against us. According to Matthew 18:15-20, we must persuade or exhort our brother. We must not only forgive but we must persuade as well. ...

"And if thy brother sin against thee" (v.15). It is quite common for God's children to sin against one another. Although such things may not happen too often, neither are they too scarce. The Lord shows us what we should do if anyone sins against us. "Go, show him his fault between thee and him alone." Should anyone sin against you, the first thing to do is to tell him, not to tell others. This is a word we should rightly understand. Show his fault to him when you and he are alone.

Day 20–Morning

Grapevines in Franschhoek, South Africa

For we know that the law is spiritual: but I am carnal, sold under sin. For that which I do I know not: for not what I would, that do I practise; but what I hate, that I do.

Romans 7:14-15

Deliverance from the Law (1)

Taken from the book: **The Glory of His Life**

In order to know how to be delivered from the law, we must first understand the relationship between the law and us. The law is God's demands on our flesh. By the law God tells us what is right and what is wrong, what we should do and what we should not do, what is forbidden and what is commanded. Hence the law is God's demands on us. Or to phrase it another way, the law is God's demands on all who are in Adam. It is His commandments to all who are in Adam as to what they ought not to do. (The purpose of God's giving the law is to prove the corruption of the flesh which is beyond cure.)

Let us remember that not only can God put us under the law, we too who are in Adam may also place ourselves under the law with a view to pleasing God. This means we may set up rules and regulations for ourselves to keep, by which we are saying: I ought not do this and I ought to do that. Besides the commandments given us by God, we also lay down commandments for ourselves to keep, and they are as strict as God's.

Consequently, we have demands on ourselves as well as God has demands on us. All this indicates that we still have hope in this man that is in Adam. We continue to expect him to strive to be better and more victorious. This, in sum, is our current situation: God puts us under the law, and we put ourselves under the law.

Day 20–Evening

African West Coast, Diaz Point, Lüderitz, Namibia

O wretched man that I am! who shall deliver me from the body of this death?

Romans 7:24 KJV

Deliverance from the Law (2)

Taken from the book: **The Glory of His Life**

What is meant by being delivered from the law? It is to be totally disillusioned about yourself. Not only to be fully disappointed, but also to expect nothing anymore. Henceforth you no longer entertain any hope in yourself. This is a being delivered from the law. God, as it were, allows you to sin day after day in order to make you realize how corrupted and unclean, how unamendable and unconquering you really are, how unable you are to keep the law because you are beyond any help. He wants you to know why He has crucified you in Christ and with Christ. It is because you are corrupted beyond cure. When you finally see yourself helpless, as well as understand that God considers you hopeless, you will then stand on the ground which God has given you. God says you are corrupted to the core and there is absolutely no hope for you; you too say you are so corrupted and helpless that you can only sin, therefore you entertain no hope in yourself. Now this is a being delivered from the law. And what a great deliverance it truly is. The one and only deliverance is a seeing yourself as being utterly hopeless. ...

Even though we know quite well in theory and in teaching that the old Adamic life is unamendable and beyond cure, yet strange to say, when it comes to experience, we still entertain hope in this Adamic life and try to amend and to improve it. Many of us are saying, I am surprised I could commit such a sin! May we be reminded that we should not be surprised at all. What sin will we not commit? We can commit any sin because the root of sin is in us. God crucified us because He saw we were, and still are, helpless and hopeless. So that when the Lord died, we too died. That God has crucified us reveals His estimate of us. Except for death or for being cast aside, we are not fit for anything.

Day 21–Morning

Lüderitz desert fishing town

Wherefore, my brethren, ye also were made dead to the law through the body of Christ; that ye should be joined to another, even to him who was raised from the dead, that we might bring forth fruit unto God.

Romans 7:4

Deliverance from the Law (3)

Taken from the book: **The Glory of His Life**

How different is our own appraisal from God's. We always think we are able and that we can. We consider ourselves capable of victory, sanctification, and progress. But God expects nothing of these from us. He declares that from head to foot our whole being is full of sins and we are altogether useless. Apart from death there is no salvation. Today we should see this basic fact of how God looks at us and what He thinks we deserve. Whoever sees this first is blessed ...

To be delivered from the law is to be delivered from God's demand, which means that, having known the work of Christ as well as the life of Adam, we give up the idea of trying to please God. As long as there is in our heart the thought of seeking progress and pleasing God by our own effort, we are not delivered from the law nor are we exempt from sorrow and despair. Knowing that God does not expect anything from us is the only way not to despair. We need to be delivered from the law; but how? It is only through death. Why is death capable of freeing us from the law? Because as long as we live, the law has its demand on us. A living person must not violate the law inasmuch as he will be prosecuted if he does. This is exactly what the apostle means by this statement: "For the woman that hath a husband is bound by law to the husband while he liveth" (Romans 7:2). If the husband still lives, the law has its claim on the woman; but if he dies, the influence of the law ceases and it demands no more. Therefore, apart from death there is no other way to be liberated from the law. For if we live, the law will keep on demanding of us.

Day 21–Evening

Fat-tailed desert sheep in Zaris, Namibia

Wherefore, my brethren, ye also were made dead to the law through the body of Christ ...

Romans 7:4a

Deliverance from the Law (4)

Taken from the book: **The Glory of His Life**

Let us go a step further and see how we die. “Wherefore, my brethren, ye also were made dead to the law through the body of Christ ...” (Romans 7:4). Our death is through the body of Christ. As Christ himself died, so we died also. The time when Christ died is when we died. Since Christ has died, we too have died. This is not committing spiritual suicide, nor do we reckon ourselves as dead, attempting to hypnotize ourselves to death. No, it is because we have seen the accomplished fact of Christ on the cross. We therefore know that God has already included us in the death of Christ. When we see this, we cannot help but acknowledge ourselves as being dead.

There are two spiritual experiences in the world which are most amazing. One is seeing God’s plan; that is to say, seeing what God has planned for you and what He designs you to be—to wit, God has sentenced you to death. The other amazing experience is seeing what God has done for you in Christ. These two spiritual facts are exceedingly great, that you can see what God has determined arbitrarily for you and also see how you are united in one with Christ, thus enjoying in Him all that He has accomplished. For instance, when Jesus Christ died on the cross you were there too, because God had included you in His death. And when His body was broken you too were broken. His crucifixion is your crucifixion, since you and Christ are one. For this reason we are careful about baptism. ...

The way of deliverance lies not in a forced reckoning of ourselves as dead. Such teaching of forced reckoning is erroneous. What, then, is the correct way? It is reckoning ourselves as dead in Christ. Not that we die ourselves, but that we were made dead through the body of Christ. Since Christ has died, and we are united with Him, therefore we too have died. The secret of victory is a never looking at ourselves outside of Christ. This is what Christ means by the words “Abide in Me” found in John 15.

Day 22–Morning

Red dune desert at Sossusvlei (basin) with extremely hardy camel thorn trees

There is therefore now no condemnation to them that are in Christ Jesus. For the law of the Spirit of life in Christ Jesus made me free from the law of sin and of death.

Romans 8:1-2

Deliverance from the Law (5)

Taken from the book: **The Glory of His Life**

It is never to look at ourselves outside of Christ. There is nothing good to be looked at outwardly, and these ugly sights cannot be improved either. If we want to look at ourselves we can only look at ourselves in the Lord. As soon as we look at the self outside of Christ we immediately fall. How often we forget the accomplished fact of Christ. We become angry with ourselves, saying, "How can I do this?" We always fail, we constantly fail. We bemoan ourselves and lose heart. Yet let us recognize the fact that all these things are done by the self that is outside of Christ. In Christ we are dead to the law. In case anyone among us has not known this deliverance, why not let that person look at himself in Christ today? In Christ God has had us crucified. He regards us as irreparable, hence there is no salvation except death. He has sentenced us to death and has also crucified us in Christ. We are now delivered from the claim of the law. We are free.

We must absolutely stand on these two facts. First, God sees that apart from death there is no other way to deliver us from the law. Second, God has already crucified us in Christ. The first speaks of God's plan, and the second, of God's work. The first is a decision, the second is an accomplishment. We have been broken into tiny fragments beyond the possibility of being made whole. Aside from death there is no salvation. Hence the foundation of redemption is in the cross. How we must accept this fact in our daily life so as to be delivered from the law. If we stand firm on this ground we will prosper. Of course you and I must confess and ask God for forgiveness when we fail. Nevertheless, we do not need to cast another look at the past since all our defeats and falls derive from the old Adamic life. Should we ask the Lord to give us strength so that we will not do it again, to men this looks excellent but to God this is unnecessary because we have died in Christ. Our history has ended, and therefore none of our decisions and desires count. How people always deem the making of a resolution to be the best thing in life, not knowing that it is like a reed which cannot withstand the enemy nor has any use before God.

Day 22–Evening

Blyde River Ravine

We were buried therefore with him through baptism unto death: that like as Christ was raised from the dead through the glory of the Father, so we also might walk in newness of life. For if we have become united with him in the likeness of his death, we shall be also in the likeness of his resurrection. Romans 6:4-5

Deliverance from the Law (6)

Taken from the book: **The Glory of His Life**

We have seen how God has crucified us with Christ. But this alone is not sufficient. So we have the following word: "... that ye should be joined to another, even to him who was raised from the dead, that we might bring forth fruit unto God" (Romans 7:4b)—and thus we have not only the negative deliverance but also the positive joining, otherwise all will still be in vain. God has not only crucified us, He has also joined us—who have been delivered from the law—to Christ, who was raised from the dead. The one is a coming out, whereas the other is an entering in. The one is the severance of a relationship, while the other is the establishing of a relationship. It is a being delivered from the law on the one hand and a being joined to Christ on the other. And this latter is what we mean by resurrection. Resurrection is a being joined with Christ, yet not the joining of one but rather the joining of many to Christ. Resurrection is the bringing of many sons into glory. This is what is alluded to in John 12: "Except a grain of wheat fall into the earth and die, it abideth by itself alone; but if it die, it beareth much fruit" (v.24). Originally there is only one life; now this life enters into many grains. Originally there is but one grain of wheat; now it has multiplied to become many grains. Likewise, Christ through death distributes His life to all believers. Thus, there are two facts in Christ: one is that God has included us in the death of Christ, and therefore when Christ died, we too died; the other is that we are raised together with Christ from the dead, thus receiving His imparted life. These are what all regenerated persons possess and possess together.

We who are resurrected in Christ will bring forth fruit to the glory of God. Since God has given the life of Christ to us, we hereafter are able to live out Christ's life. Whatever be the grain of wheat that is sown, there shall be the thirty, the sixty or the hundred grains which grow out of it. If a person plants barley he will not get wheat or squash. What is sown is that which grows. There can be no change. If what is sown is wheat, all which grows out will be wheat. How can we live like Christ and bear fruit to glorify God as Christ did? In only one way: by letting Christ live in us and letting Him live out of us. Consequently, Christ not only died for us on the cross but He also lives for us within us. Who can make us live like Christ? None except the One who gives the life of Christ to us. As we have the life of Christ, we may bear fruit to the glory of God.

Day 23–Morning

The African wild green pigeon

Howbeit when he, the Spirit of truth, is come, he shall guide you into all the truth …
He shall glorify me: for he shall take of mine, and shall declare it unto you.

John 16:13-14

Spiritual Reality

Taken from the book: **Worship God**

Oftentimes spiritual reality is nothing more than terminology to us for we have not yet entered into the reality of it. Only after we have entered in can we touch that which is real. Hence the question becomes, How can we enter into spiritual reality? "Howbeit when he, the Spirit of truth, is come, he shall guide you into all the truth ... He shall glorify me: for he shall take of mine, and shall declare it unto you" (John 16:13-14). ...

Spiritual progress is not a question of attaining to some abstract standard, not a question of pressing through to some far-off goal; it is wholly a question of seeing God's standard. Spiritual progress comes by finding out what you really are, not by trying to be what you hope to be. You will never reach that goal, however earnestly you strive. It is when you see you are dead that you die; it is when you see you are risen that you rise; it is when you see you are holy that you become holy. It is seeing the goal that determines the pathway to the goal. The goal is revealed by inward seeing, not by desiring or by working. There is only one possibility of spiritual progress, and that is by discovering God's facts. Our great need is just to see the truth as God sees it—the truth concerning Christ, the truth concerning ourselves in Christ, and the truth concerning the Church, the Body of Christ. ...

The Church is not a company of Christians working their way heavenward, but a company of Christians who are actually now citizens of heaven. Alas! Christianity in the experience of most Christians is an endeavor to be what they are not, and an endeavor to do what they cannot do. They are always struggling to not love the world because at heart they really love it. They are always trying to be humble because at heart they are still proud. This is the experience of so-called Christianity, but it is not the experience of the Church.

Day 23–Evening

Damara Tern in the wetlands of Walvis Bay

I have been crucified with Christ; and it is no longer I that live, but Christ living in me: and that life which I now live in the flesh I live in faith, the faith which is in the Son of God, who loved me, and gave himself up for me. Galatians 2:20

To Live Is Christ

Taken from the book: **The Salvation of the Soul**

Now we know that only Christ is victorious. We also know that He lives in us. For when we believe in Him, we have Him. Yet day by day I am still myself as though nothing had happened. What should we do in order that Christ may live out His life in us? There are two ways, or may we say that there are two conditions. First, surrender. Yes, Christ is indeed in me, but He cannot do anything if I do not let Him. You and I must obey God. What precisely is surrender? Surrender is not a promising God to do His will, nor is it making covenant with God to do what cannot be done. To surrender is for me to take my hands off my own life. It is to give over into God's hand my good and bad, my strength and weakness, my past and future, my very life and very self so that God alone may work in me. ...

The second way or condition for Christ to be able to live out His life in us is to believe. Since we have surrendered, we must now believe that God will deliver us from what we love, what we cannot and will not give up. "Commit thy way unto Jehovah; trust also in him, and he will bring it to pass" (Psalm 37:5). To commit is to surrender; to trust is to believe. And the result is that "he will bring it to pass." Knowing that we have no way, we commit ourselves to God and believe that the Lord who dwells in us will accomplish the work.

Can you say, I am victorious? Hallelujah, I can say I am victorious, because the Bible tells me so. How pitiful that our faith is less than the size of a grain of mustard—nay, even less than a speck of dust! If we have faith, God will begin to work. When the Lord created the heavens and the earth He merely used His mouth, for when He said "Let there be light" there was light! If we have faith, He most certainly will begin to work because He is anxious to have His work done. ...

Day 24–Morning

Windhoek area, Central Namibia

Neither present your members unto sin as instruments of unrighteousness; but present yourselves unto God, as alive from the dead, and your members as instruments of righteousness unto God. Romans 6:13

Surrender and Faith

Taken from the book: **The Salvation of the Soul**

We need to see that surrender and faith are intimately related. When these two actions are joined together, there is victory and no defeat. We will have no victory if we merely believe and yet are unwilling to give our lives to God in exchange for the life of Christ. Though at the time of regeneration we have already come into possession of this life of Christ, God will not force us to live by the life of Christ if our will is not surrendered to God to let Christ live in and out through us. And by the same token, if we only surrender but do not believe, such surrender will be reduced to a kind of dead work; for although we are prepared to give God the right to work, we have not given Him the opportunity to come in.

Hence we must (1) lift up our head to look to God and say, I hand over my all to You, I am willing to let You work; and (2) believe that God has already worked according to His word.

Christ has taken care of all the conflicts, for the divine government is upon His shoulders. Let us believe Him day by day, because faith needs to be continued whereas surrender is done once and for all. We may surrender to God in one instant and need never do it again. (Though some people surrender gradually and slowly, this is unnecessary.) Having committed ourselves to God in surrender, we believe He will cause Christ to live His holiness and victory in and through us. Formerly we were saved from the punishment of hell; now we are saved from the power of sin. Nothing needs to be done except surrender and believe. May we prove that we are truly victorious.

Day 24–Evening

Walvis Bay Jetty

And also the Strength of Israel [margin, “the Victory of Israel”] will not lie nor repent; for he is not a man, that he should repent.

I Samuel 15:29

Victory (1)

Taken from the book: **The Life that Wins**

"The Strength of Israel [margin, "the Victory of Israel"] will not lie nor repent; for he is not a man, that he should repent" (I Samuel 15:29). The first mention of victory in the whole Bible is found in I Samuel 15:29. There it says that Victory will not lie nor repent. The Victory of Israel is neither an experience nor an event; it is a Person. I am sure we all know who that Person is. It is Christ! Hence let me tell you today that victory does not reside in ourselves, nor is it our own experience. Victory is not you as the problem; victory is the person of Christ living for you! And thus the victory we obtain will neither lie nor repent. Praise God, victory is a living Person! According to the word of God, the nature of victorious life is many-sided...

First of all, please notice that victory is an exchanged life, not a changed life. Victory is not that I have changed, but rather that I have been exchanged. One verse which is most familiar to us is Galatians 2:20: "I have been crucified with Christ; and it is no longer I that live, but Christ liveth in me: and that life which I now live in the flesh I live in faith, the faith which is in the Son of God." What is meant by this verse? It has only one meaning: the life spoken of is an exchanged life. Basically, it is no longer I, for it has absolutely nothing to do with me. It is not that the bad I has become the good I, or the unclean I has changed to be the clean I. It is simply "not I." Today people make a serious mistake in thinking that victory is progressive and defeat is retrogressive—that if a person is able to control his temper or maintain an intimate fellowship with God, then he is victorious. Not so. Let us ever keep in mind that victory has basically no relation to one's own self...

Day 25–Morning

True desert beauty of the Namib Desert

Blessed be the God and Father of our Lord Jesus Christ, who hath blessed us with every spiritual blessing in the heavenly places in Christ.

Ephesians 1:3

Victory (2)

Taken from the book: **The Life that Wins**

There is one thing we must understand in all this, which is, that victory is a gift and not a reward. What is a gift? It is something which is freely given to you. That which you earn through work is a reward. A gift, on the other hand, asks for no effort on your part. It is that which is given gratuitously with no requirement placed upon the receiver, whereas a reward demands that someone work for it. The life that wins which we talk about does not require any effort of yours: "thanks be to God, who giveth us the victory through our Lord Jesus Christ" (I Corinthians 15:57). Victory is something which God has prepared to give to us. Our victory is obtained freely, not attained through self-effort.

Too often we believers have a serious misconception—imagining that while salvation comes to us freely, victory depends on ourselves. We know we cannot add any merit or work of ours to obtain salvation. We must simply come to the cross and accept the Lord Jesus as our Saviour. This is the gospel! We realize we cannot be saved by works, yet we reason that for sanctification we must do good works after we are saved. This is to say that though you cannot be saved by works, you need to depend on works for victory. Let me tell you that just as you are not saved by works, so you do not overcome by works. God has declared that you are unable to do good. Christ has died for you on the cross, and He is now living for you within. That which is of the flesh is flesh, and God rejects all that came from it. Nevertheless, we usually surmise that while salvation is dependent upon the substitutionary death of Christ on the cross, we should think of doing good, should do good, and expect to do good for victory in our lives. Let us realize, though, that we can do no good. Victory is freely given us by God!

Day 25–Evening

A Kalahari Steenbok, a member of the Dwarf Antelope family, the Neotragini

For whom the Lord loveth he chasteneth, and scourgeth every son whom he receiveth.

Hebrews 12:6

The Discipline of the Lord

Taken from the book: **Love One Another**

"For whom the Lord loveth he chasteneth, and scourgeth every son whom he receiveth" (v.6). This is quoted from Proverbs 3:12. It shows us the "why" of all chastenings. God does not deal with everyone in the world. He only chastens those whom He loves. He chastens us because we are His beloved. He wants to make us into a suitable vessel. That is why He spends time on His children to chasten them. Chastisement, then, is love's arrangement. Love arranges these happenings. Love measures what we should meet. Love plans the details of our environment. We call this discipline because it always aims at the highest good and the ultimate intention of creation. "And scourgeth every son whom he receiveth." Those who are chastened of the Lord are those who are assuredly accepted by God. To be scourged is not a sign of rejection, but rather the evidence of God's special approval. God does not deal with everyone; He just concentrates on dealing with those whom He loves, those who are accepted as His sons. ...

After you become a Christian, you will see the hand of God leading you. Many prearranged things will happen to you. Scourgings will come too. Why the scourgings? Because whenever you are not walking in God's appointed way, you will be scourged and urged to turn from that direction back to the appointed road. Every child of God must be prepared to accept this disciplinary hand of God. Because you are His son, He chastens you. If you are not His beloved, He will not make the effort to discipline you. Thus, to be chastened and scourged is an indication that we are loved and accepted by God. Only Christians share in His chastening and scourging. What we receive is not punishment but discipline. Punishment serves the purpose of repaying the wrong, but discipline has an educational purpose. Punishment deals only with the past—one is scourged because he has done wrong. Discipline has an eye toward the future though it also deals with past faults. Discipline, therefore, has these two elements—an educational purpose as training for the future. As soon as one comes to Christ and belongs to the Lord, he should be prepared to let God mold him into a vessel of honor.

Day 26–Morning

Steppe Eagle, in the Bushveld

Finally, be strong in the Lord, and in the strength of his might. Put on the whole armor of God, that ye may be able to stand against the wiles of the devil.

Ephesians 6:10-11

Spiritual Warfare (1)

Taken from the book: **Let Us Pray**

The most important thing before us now is to identify the enemy. We should know for sure who is our adversary, who it is that causes us much suffering. How frequently we account our sufferings to be from men. But the Bible tells us that "our wrestling is not against flesh and blood, but against the principalities, against the powers, against the world-rulers of this darkness, against the spiritual hosts of wickedness in the heavenly places" (Ephesians 6:12). Hence every time we suffer from the hand of man, we need to remember that behind flesh and blood Satan and his powers of darkness can very well be there directing everything. We should have the necessary spiritual insight to discern the work of God from the maneuver of Satan at the back of everything. We should distinguish what is natural and what is supernatural. We should be so inwardly exercised as to gain knowledge of the spiritual realm so that none of Satan's hidden work can escape our observation.

Such being the case, shall we not recognize that what we usually consider to be incidental and natural happenings may involve the works of the enemy behind the scenes? We shall readily see that Satan is really trying to frustrate us at every turn and oppress us in all things. What a pity we have suffered so much from him in the past without knowing that it was he who made us suffer. Now part of the most urgent work of ours today is to generate a heart of hatred towards Satan for his cruelty. We do not need to be fearful lest our enmity towards Satan becomes too deep. Before there is the possibility of our overcoming we must maintain in our heart a hostile attitude towards him, no longer willing to subject ourselves to his oppression. We ought to understand that what we have suffered at Satan's hands is a real grievance which must be avenged. He has no right to harass us, yet he does it anyway. This is indeed an injustice, a grievance which cannot remain unavenged.

Day 26–Evening

A lonely deserted house in the Namib Desert

And he shall speak words against the Most High,
and shall wear out the saints of the Most High.

Daniel 7:25a

Spiritual Warfare (2)

Taken from the book: **Let Us Pray**

Satan has a work, which is attacking the children of God. His attack may not come suddenly; oftentimes, it comes gradually and slowly. Daniel 7:25 mentions how Satan shall wear out the saints of the Most High. Satan has in fact a plan against the saints of the Most High, which is to wear them out. Hence let us clearly recognize that the work of Satan in the lives of God's children is frequently not very noticeable, since his work is slowly to wear them down.

What is the meaning of the phrase, "wear out"? It has in it the idea of reducing a little this minute, then reducing a little further the next minute. Reduce a little today and reduce a little more tomorrow. Thus the wearing out is almost imperceptible; nevertheless, it is a reducing. The wearing down is scarcely an activity of which one is conscious, yet the end result is that there is nothing left. Hence this principle of Satan's working in the lives of God's children is to wear them out until they are worn down completely. He will wear you out a little today and then a little more the next day. He will make you suffer a small amount now and a little more later. You may think this to be something insignificant, nevertheless Satan knows that the consequence of such wearing away is to wear the saint out completely.

For this reason, the Bible indicates that "the love of the many shall wax cold" (Matthew 24:12), which means a gradually growing cold. It also mentions how a certain maid, having a spirit of divination, cried out after Paul and his colleagues for many days (see Acts 16:17-18). Moreover, the Scriptures record that when Felix hoped that Paul would give him money, he sent for Paul the oftener and communed with him (Acts 24:26). And the Old Testament also describes how Delilah pressed Samson daily with her word and so urged him continually that his soul was vexed unto death (Judges 16:16). Such is how Satan gradually, and for many days, will frequently wear out the children of God. "The evil day" spoken of in Ephesians 6:13 refers to the wearing-out tactics of Satan. We must ask God to open our eyes that we may discern how Satan would wear us out and how we should combat his wearing-out tactic.

Day 27–Morning

A desert ostrich cooling in the shade of a camel thorn tree

Be sober, be watchful: your adversary the devil, as a roaring lion, walketh about, seeking whom he may devour.

I Peter 5:8

Spiritual Warfare (3)

Taken from the book: **Let Us Pray**

Satan also wears out your spiritual life. He will take away your prayer life little by little, and cause you to trust God less and less and yourself more and more, a little at a time. He will make you feel somewhat cleverer than before. Step by step you are misled to rely more on your own gift, and step by step your heart is enticed away from the Lord. ...

Satan will also wear out our time..... If the children of God do not discern Satan's wiles they can easily fall into his trap. How we must redeem our time and make every hour count. ...

God's children should therefore rise up to repudiate and reprove the enemy. Some people fail to get relieved because they still have "strength" to endure. A person who keeps on enduring Satanic wear and tear, allowing the devil to waste away his energy, his joy and his spiritual life, has fallen into the wile of the enemy. Let us be clear, of course, that we should not be angry at the people who are used by Satan; on the contrary, we ought to be patient with them, even loving them. But we must oppose and resist the hidden conspiracy of Satan. If we withstand what he does, we will soon be freed. ...

Why are the minds of so many Christians confused? It is because they are always resisting. "Resist the devil, and he will flee from you," says the Bible. Resist him once, and he will flee. You ought to believe that he has fled away. You do not need to resist him many times. Simply believe that he has fled, for this is in accordance with God's word. Whatever then comes back is not true. You can well afford to ignore it, and, if you do, it will soon disappear. It lurks just outside the door, trying to peep in; if you reckon it as true, it will immediately step in. So, the basic principle is: resist the first time, ignore the second time.

Day 27–Evening

A rocky mountain top towards the end of the Dragon Mountains

Now is come the salvation, and the power, and the kingdom of our God, and the authority of his Christ: for the accuser of our brethren is cast down, who accuseth them before our God day and night. Revelation 12:10

Spiritual Warfare (4)

Taken from the book: **Love One Another**

Satan not only attacks the mind and the body but also the conscience. This attack is what we call accusation. It causes great distress to the Christian who feels himself at fault and thus unable to rise up before God. Accusation may weaken one's whole being. Many dare not resist for fear that it may be the reproof of the Holy Spirit. ...

What is the difference between a conscience under accusation and the reproach of the Holy Spirit? It is extremely important that we know the difference. Satan's accusation is never clear and sharp, whereas the revelation from God distinctly places your sin before you. ...

Furthermore, Satanic accusation lacks positive purpose. It does not edify you but, instead, causes you to suffer. It mumbles till it affects you and so overwhelms you that you are no longer able to stand up before God. The purpose of the reproach of the Holy Spirit, however, is to strengthen you, not to weaken you. The more you are reproved, the easier for you to rise up before God. Satanic accusation produces the opposite effect: the more you are accused, the more you are weakened. Hence the reproach of the Holy Spirit is positive in nature. He so reproves that you have to go to the Lord and learn your lesson. Satanic accusation is quite different. It keeps accusing you until you have been crushed and become useless.

Furthermore, the results of Satanic accusation are very different from the results of the reproach of the Holy Spirit. If it is the reproach of the Holy Spirit, you will have joy, and at the very least, peace within you after you have confessed your sin. At the time you are reproved, you do suffer agony; but as soon as you confess your sin before God, you enjoy peace in your heart. Sometimes you will be filled with joy, for the heavy burden has been lifted. With Satanic accusation it is not so. Even at the time of prayer and confession, you are still bothered by his mumbling. He will insinuate that you are sinful and useless, that your confession before God is of no avail, that you will be just as weak after asking for forgiveness as you were before. These are sure signs that the accusation is of Satan; it is not the reproach of the Holy Spirit ...

Do keep it well in mind that through the blood of the Lord our conscience may be purified. No sin in the world is so great that the blood cannot cleanse it. Satan, though, will attempt to weaken our conscience to such an extent that we wonder if the blood of our Lord is able to cleanse us. We feel as though we could never be forgiven. This is indeed a Satanic accusation, a lie of the devil .

Day 28–Morning

Even in the desert His mercies are new every morning.

And they overcame him because of the blood of the Lamb, and because of the word of their testimony; and they loved not their life even unto death.

Revelation 12:11

Spiritual Warfare (5)

Taken from the book: **Love One Another**

How do Christians overcome? "Because of the blood of the Lamb" (Revelation 12:11). Through the death of the Lord Jesus, we are united with God into one. The primary objective of Satanic attack is to separate us from God. As long as we are one with God, Satan has absolutely no way to injure us. What, then, separates us from God? Sin alone separates us, but the blood of Jesus, God's Son, cleanses us from all our sins.

Revelation 12:11 tells us that the brethren overcame Satan because of the blood of the Lamb. With the cleansing of the blood of the Lord Jesus, we are made one with God. When we have the consciousness of sin upon our conscience, we are instantly separated from Him. As soon as the consciousness of sin comes upon us, the devil begins his attack. Without such consciousness he has no way to launch his assault. Thank God, the blood of the Lamb has overcome Satan. Today even the feeblest of God's children can overcome Satan, for every one of us has the blood.

You may not have many other things, but the blood you definitely do have. Through the blood of the Lord Jesus, you quite naturally declare that all your sins have been cleansed. Today God is your God. If God is for you, who can be against you? With your God by your side, the devil cannot attack you. The reason why he is able to accuse and attack is because he has first implanted a consciousness of sin in us. But the blood has placed you on God's side, so Satan cannot do anything with you.

Remember well that once the conscience is purified from the consciousness of sins, Satan can no longer stage his attack. The blood of the Lamb overcomes him. Is it not an amazing thing that whenever man comes before God he senses his unworthiness, but when he confronts Satan he feels guilty? Such a guilty feeling makes him susceptible to the hand of the enemy. So he needs at that moment to declare, "I am sinful; that is why you attack me. But through the blood of the Lamb I overcome you. The Lord Jesus has died for me; His blood has been shed. What can you do to me?" Let us therefore believe. Believe that the Lord was manifested to destroy the works of the devil. Believe that the Lord's death has spelled destruction to Satan's attack.

Day 28–Evening

African White-backed Vulture in the Lowveld

Behold, I have given you authority to tread upon serpents and scorpions, and over all the power of the enemy: and nothing shall in any wise hurt you.

Luke 10:19

Spiritual Warfare (6)

Taken from the book: **Love One Another**

"Be subject therefore unto God; but resist the devil, and he will flee from you." (James 4:7)

I hope brothers and sisters understand what is meant by resisting. Satan is a defeated foe; he is a fugitive, a prisoner who should have been totally eliminated on the cross of our Lord. Today is only the day of his escape. When the kingdom comes, he shall be completely destroyed. So today he does not tempt in open warfare; rather, he hides outside the door behind the wall to sneak in with his temptation. He does everything secretly. When that happens, do not forget that you represent the Lord God and that Satan is but a fugitive tempting you outside the wall, not inside the room. You need not be afraid of him nor resist him as though he were part of the regular army. You should announce to him, "You are completely defeated!

You were done for at the cross! You ought to have been eliminated, but were not; hence your coming today is not permitted!" The Bible states clearly that if you withstand, Satan will flee from you. He is a fugitive today, trying to deceive you at the door. You should tell him who he is; then he will run away. If you think of him as already being in your home, then you will certainly be disturbed. He comes only to deceive and to try you. If he cannot succeed, he will flee from you.

Day 29–Morning

Kalahari Sunset

Ye ask, and receive not, because ye ask amiss, that ye may spend it in your pleasures.

James 4:3

Prayer (1)

Taken from the book: **Let Us Pray**

A serious error concerning prayer prevails in our common understanding, which is to say, that we often think of prayer as an outlet for expressing what we need—as our cry to God for help. We do not see that prayer is the asking of God to fulfill His needs. We ought to understand that God's original thought is certainly not the letting of believers achieve their own aims through prayer, rather is it God accomplishing His purpose through the prayers of the believers. This is not meant to imply that Christians should never ask the Lord to supply their needs. It only is meant to indicate how we need first to understand the meaning and principles of prayer. ...

True prayer is a real work. Praying according to God's will and praying only for His will is indeed a self-denying work. Unless we are completely weaned from ourselves, having not the slightest interest of our own but living absolutely for the Lord and seeking only His glory, we will not like what He likes, nor seek what He seeks, nor pray what He wants us to pray. Without doubt, to work for God with no self-interest is very difficult; but to pray for Him without any self-interest is even harder. Even so, all who live for God must do this. ...

When God works, He does so with specific law and definite principle. Even though He could do whatever pleases Him, yet he never acts carelessly. He always performs according to His determinate law and principle. Unquestionably He can transcend all these laws and principles, for He is God and is quite capable of acting according to His own pleasure. Nonetheless, we discover a most marvelous fact in the Bible; which is, that in spite of His exceeding greatness and His ability to operate according to His will, God ever acts along the line of the law or principle which He has laid down. It seems as though He deliberately puts himself under the law to be controlled by His own law.

Day 29–Evening

A desert road at Augrabies after wonderful rains

With all prayer and supplication praying at all seasons in the Spirit, and watching thereunto in all perseverance and supplication for all the saints.

Ephesians 6:18

Prayer (2)

Taken from the book: **Let Us Pray**

There was once a Christian who well knew how to pray. He declared this, that all spiritual works include four steps: The first step is that God conceives a thought, which is His will: The second step is that God reveals this will to His children through the Holy Spirit, causing them to know that He has a will, a plan, a demand and expectation: The third step is that God's children return His will by praying to Him, for prayer is responding to God's will—if our heart is wholly one with His heart, we will naturally voice in our prayer what He intends to do: And the fourth step is that God will accomplish this very thing.

How should we lay tracks for the will of God? The answer: "With all prayer and supplication praying at all seasons in the Spirit" (Ephesians 6:18). Our prayer should touch in many directions. We should pray constantly. Pray specific prayers as well as general ones. Many of our prayers are too thinly spread; there are too many holes by which Satan is given plenty of opportunities to slip in. Were our prayers well-rounded and tightly guarded, he would have no chance to do havoc. ...

There is one particular secret about prayer that we should know about, which is, a praying three times to the Lord. This "thrice" is not limited to only three times, it may be many times. The Lord Jesus asked God three times in the garden of Gethsemane until His prayer was heard—at which point He stopped. Paul too prayed to God three times, and ceased praying after he was given God's word. Hence all prayers should heed the principle of thrice. This "thrice" does not mean that we need only pray once, twice, and three times, and then stop. It simply signifies the fact that before we stop we must pray thoroughly until God hears us.

Day 30–Morning

Lüderitz Harbor

Let us therefore draw near with boldness unto the throne of grace, that we may receive mercy, and may find grace to help us in time of need.

Hebrews 4:16

Prayer (3)

Taken from the books: **The Prayer Ministry of the Church & God's Plan and the Overcomers**

Finally, a serious thing is in order here; which is, that we must ourselves be subject to the authority of God. Except we are in subjection to God's authority we cannot exercise authoritative prayer. ...

Authoritative prayer is not petitioning, it is commanding; for there are two kinds of prayer: not only the prayer of petition but also the prayer of command: "Command ye me" says Isaiah 45:11. We may command God to do things, and such is commanding prayer.

Commanding prayer commences at the ascension of Christ. The death and resurrection of Christ, as we have seen, resolves God's four cardinal issues—so that His death concludes all that is in Adam, His resurrection gives us new ground, and His ascension makes us sit in the heavenly places far above all rule and authority and power and dominion and every name that is named: not only in this world but also in that which is to come. Ephesians 1 is a record of the ascension of Christ who ascended far above all rule and authority. Ephesians 2 tells of our sitting with Christ in the heavenly places. As Christ is far above all rule and authority, so we also are above all rule and authority.

Ephesians 1 tells us that the position of Christ is in the heavenly places. Chapter 2 tells us that our place in Christ is sitting with Him in the heavenly places. Chapter 6 tells us what we do in the heavenly places, even sitting there and praying—that is to say, exercising the authority of Christ and giving out commanding prayers. Ordinary prayer is a praying from earth to heaven. Commanding prayer is a praying from heaven to earth. The prayer in Matthew 6 is petitionary prayer, and hence is upward in direction. The prayer in Ephesians 6 is commanding prayer, and therefore it is downward. Thus we sit in the heavenly places and pour forth commanding prayer. "Amen" in Hebrew means "So be it" or "So it is"—this is command. At the beginning of any warfare Satan tries to unseat us from our heavenly position, which is one of victory. Warfare is a battle for position. Hence victory lies in occupying the right place. Being in Christ and sitting in the heavenly places alone gives authoritative prayer.

Day 30–Evening

Bright pink Flamingos in the pink-algae rich wetlands of Walvis Bay

Through him then let us offer up a sacrifice of praise to God continually, that is, the fruit of lips which make confession to his name.

Hebrews 13:15

Praise

Taken from the book: **Assembling Together**

God wants men today to offer praise as if offering a sacrifice. In other words, He enables you to offer praises to Him by wounding you, grinding you, and cutting you deeply. God's throne is established on praises. How will He obtain these praises?—by His children's coming to Him, each bringing the sacrifice of praise. ...

First we need to see that praise is a sacrifice. Then we shall see that it is also a way to victory. It is a very common strategy of Satan to attack God's children in the area of prayer. Many brothers and sisters complain to me that they are so frequently under attack they cannot pray very well. We often read in spiritual books that what Satan fears most is God's children in prayer, that he will flee when God's children are on their knees. This is quite familiar to us. But what I would like to say today is, that what Satan attacks most furiously is not prayer, but praise. I do not say Satan does not attack prayer. When a Christian starts to pray, Satan begins to attack. It is therefore relatively easy to talk with people, but quite difficult to pray. Indeed, Satan does attack prayer. However, he also assaults the praise of God's children. If he could prevent all words of praise from rising up to God, he would gladly use all his strength to do so.

Do remember: whenever God's children are praising, Satan must flee. Prayer frequently is a battle, but praise is victory. Prayer is spiritual warfare; praise is the shout of triumph. For this reason praise is that which Satan hates most. He will exert all his strength to quench our praise whenever possible. The children of God act foolishly when they look at their environment or consider their feelings and then stop praising the Lord. If they really know God, they will see that even in the jail at Philippi there was a place for song. As Paul and Silas were praying and singing hymns unto God, all the doors of the prison opened (Acts 16:25-26). Prayer may not always open prison doors but praise does!

Day 31–Morning

A sheep and cattle stone corral wall in the Freestate

That ye may become blameless and harmless, children of God without blemish in the midst of a crooked and perverse generation, among whom ye are seen as lights in the world. Philippians 2:15

Separation from the World (1)

Taken from the book: **The Good Confession**

Nonetheless, we must remember that to be redeemed by the blood is to be delivered from the world. Once redeemed, instantly we become pilgrims and sojourners on earth. This does not imply that we no longer live on earth; it simply means we are instantaneously separated from the world. Wherever there is redemption, there is separation. The blood divides the living and the dead; the blood separates God's children from the people of the world. The redeemed are no longer permanent residents of this world. ...

We Christians must come out of the world as a system. To be separated from the world means to be separated from this world system in its moral connotation. It does not imply leaving the world as a place.

D. M. Panton has a well-spoken word concerning our walk in the wilderness. He says: in life, it is a way; in death, it is a tomb. No one can remain in this world too long, for it is only a way. It also serves as a grave when one dies. This should be our attitude towards the world. Every believer must be separated. In the eyes of the people of this world, we are but strangers and sojourners in the wilderness; they alone are the permanent residents of the world ...

We must be separated from anything the world considers unworthy of a Christian. We start our Christian life before the world and the world sets up certain standards for Christians. If we cannot measure up to their standards, where will our testimony be? Of the things which we do, we should never permit non-believers to raise their eyebrows saying, "Do Christians do such things too?" Under such an accusation, our testimony before them is finished ...

Anything which is inconsistent to our relationship with the Lord must be rejected. Our Lord was humiliated on earth; can we seek for glory? He was crucified as a robber; can we court the favor of this world? He was slandered as possessed of a demon; can we look for praise from men that we are most clever and rational? Such conditions reveal the inconsistency of our relationship with the Lord. They make us different from the Lord, even contrary to Him. All the ways which He has gone we also must walk through. For this cause we must eradicate everything that is inconsistent to our relationship with the Lord.

Day 31–Evening

A hazy day in the desert near the Tropic of Capricorn in West Namibia

Know ye not that the friendship of the world is enmity with God? Whosoever therefore would be a friend of the world maketh himself an enemy of God.

James 4:4

Separation from the World (2)

Taken from the book: **The Good Confession**

Again we ask, "What is the world?" Each and everything which tends to quench our spiritual life before the Lord is the world. How impossible it is to tell new believers what things are permissible and what things are not permissible. If we tell them ten things, they have the eleventh thing to ask. But if they understand but one principle, they can apply it to numberless things. Whatsoever thing makes you lose zeal for prayer or for Bible reading or causes you to lose courage to testify is the world. The world creates a kind of atmosphere which cools our love to the Lord. It withers our spiritual life; it chills our zeal; it freezes our longing for God. Hence it must be rejected...

Another thing to be mentioned is concerned with social relationships. Whatever social gatherings or feasts or good times together cause our lamp to be covered under a bushel are of the world. These should be rejected. How can Christians continue in social intercourse if they cannot confess that they are the Lord's and if they have to pretend to be polite by listening to and smiling with unbelievers? How can we suppress our inward feeling and put on a smiling face?

... Whatever thing causes the conscience of weak believers to stumble is to be taken as the world. At the outset we mentioned things condemned by the world as unworthy of Christians; now we speak of things condemned by feeble Christians. Notice these are not things disapproved of by strong Christians; rather they are reprehended by weak Christians. As a matter of fact, these weak believers may not be correct in their judgment. What they disapprove of may be quite all right. Yet they have a weak conscience just as once we did. How can I stumble them in the things which they consider wrong? I must walk before them as without any offense. "All things are lawful for me; but not all things are expedient" (I Corinthians 6:12), says Paul. All things are lawful, for from our standpoint these things are not of the world; but to feeble Christians they are things of the world. Consequently, we must for their sake refrain from them.

Christian Fellowship Publishers

Sunrise over the Indian Ocean at Kosi Bay

www.c-f-p.com | 804-794-5333

Titles Available by Watchman Nee

Aids to "Revelation"
Amazing Grace
Back to the Cross
A Balanced Christian Life
The Better Covenant
The Body of Christ: A Reality
The Character of God's Workman
Christ the Sum of All Spiritual Things
The Church and the Work – 3 Vols
The Church in the Eternal Purpose of God
"Come, Lord Jesus"
The Communion of the Holy Spirit
The Finest of the Wheat – Vol. 1
The Finest of the Wheat – Vol. 2
From Faith to Faith
From Glory to Glory
Full of Grace and Truth – Vol. 1
Full of Grace and Truth – Vol. 2
Gleanings in the Fields of Boaz
The Glory of His Life
God's Plan and the Overcomers
God's Work
Gospel Dialogue
Grace for Grace
Heart to Heart Talks
Interpreting Matthew
Journeying towards the Spiritual
The King and the Kingdom of Heaven
The Latent Power of the Soul
Let Us Pray
The Life That Wins
The Lord My Portion
The Messenger of the Cross
The Ministry of God's Word
My Spiritual Journey
The Mystery of Creation
Powerful According to God
Practical Issues of This Life
The Prayer Ministry of the Church
The Release of the Spirit
Revive Thy Work
The Salvation of the Soul
The Secret of Christian Living
Serve in Spirit
The Spirit of Judgment
The Spirit of the Gospel
The Spirit of Wisdom and Revelation
Spiritual Authority
Spiritual Discernment
Spiritual Exercise
Spiritual Knowledge
The Spiritual Man
Spiritual Reality or Obsession
Take Heed
The Testimony of God
The Universal Priesthood of Believers
Whom Shall I Send?
The Word of the Cross
Worship God
Ye Search the Scriptures

The Basic Lesson Series

Vol. 1 - A Living Sacrifice
Vol. 2 - The Good Confession
Vol. 3 - Assembling Together
Vol. 4 - Not I, But Christ
Vol. 5 - Do All to the Glory of God
Vol. 6 - Love One Another

Christian Fellowship Publishers

A Hartlaub's Seagull in Namaqueland, West Coast, in the fishing village Paternoster

Titles Available by Stephen Kaung

The Key to "Revelation" Volumes I and II

"But We See Jesus"
—the Life of the Lord Jesus

Discipled to Christ
—As Seen in the Life of Simon Peter

God's Purpose for the Family

The Gymnasium of Christ

In the Footsteps of Christ

New Covenant Living & Ministry

Now We See the Church
—the Life of the Church, the Body of Christ

Shepherding

The Songs of Degrees
—Meditations on Fifteen Psalms

The Splendor of His Ways
—Seeing the Lord's End in Job

<u>The "God Has Spoken" Series</u>

Seeing Christ in the Old Testament, Part One

Seeing Christ in the Old Testament, Part Two

Seeing Christ in the New Testament